NEW DIRECTIONS
FOR
PHILANTHROPIC
FUNDRAISING

Cathlene Williams
Association of Fundraising Professionals

Lilya Wagner
The Center on Philanthropy at Indiana University
COEDITORS-IN-CHIEF

EXPLORING THE RELATIONSHIP BETWEEN VOLUNTEERS AND FUNDRAISERS

Rebecca E. Hunter
American Thoracic Society

EDITOR

NUMBER 39, SPRING 2003

Exploring the Relationship Between Volunteers and Fundraisers
Rebecca E. Hunter (ed.)
New Directions for Philanthropic Fundraising, No. 39, Spring 2003
Cathlene Williams, Lilya Wagner, Coeditors-in-chief

NEW DIRECTIONS FOR PHILANTHROPIC FUNDRAISING is indexed in Higher Education Abstracts and Philanthropic Index.

Microfilm copies of issues and articles are available in 16 mm and 35 mm, as well as microfiche in 105 mm, through University Microfilms Inc., 300 North Zeeb Road, Ann Arbor, Michigan 48106-1346.

ISSN 1072-172X (print)   ISSN 1542-7846 (online)

NEW DIRECTIONS FOR PHILANTHROPIC FUNDRAISING is part of the Jossey-Bass Nonprofit and Public Management Series and is published quarterly by Wiley Subscription Services, Inc., A Wiley company, at Jossey-Bass, 989 Market Street, San Francisco, California 94103-1741.

SUBSCRIPTIONS cost $99.00 for individuals and $199.00 for institutions, agencies, and libraries. Prices subject to change. Refer to the order form at the back of this issue.

EDITORIAL CORRESPONDENCE should be sent to Lilya Wagner, The Center on Philanthropy, Indiana University, 550 West North Street, Suite 301, Indianapolis, IN 46202-3162, or to Cathlene Williams, Association of Fundraising Professionals, 1101 King Street, Suite 700, Alexandria, VA 22314.

www.josseybass.com

Contents

Editor's Notes

UNLESS SOMEONE HAS come up with an entirely new theory about fundraising within the last ten minutes, I believe all financial development professionals agree that our work revolves around developing strong people relationships. Even corporate and foundation resources are secured through the relationship with the individual or individuals representing the funder.

Volunteers traditionally have been involved in garnering philanthropic gifts since the first solicitations conducted in the colonies over two centuries ago.

Now, in the twenty-first century, American society has changed dramatically. American traditions are melded within myriad cultures. Are volunteers still relevant to the fundraiser's work? If so, for what reasons? If not, why not?

This volume of *New Directions for Philanthropic Fundraising* looks atypically at volunteers and fundraising. Contributing authors examine fewer of the how-tos of working with volunteers and more of the psychological and psychosocial aspects of volunteers' and development professionals' personalities. The assessment extends to organizational characteristics, evolutionary stage and size, and the reasons that certain types of volunteers and fundraisers may be drawn to work with a particular nonprofit group.

Why would anyone, volunteer or paid, willingly involve him- or herself in fundraising? Sometimes, I am certain, we all question our decision. Often this profession picks us. Some opt to stay and some opt to change careers.

The volume is organized in a logical progression from broad concept to microcosm. In Chapter One, Bruce Bonnicksen addresses the new roles of volunteers in development. His primary

NEW DIRECTIONS FOR PHILANTHROPIC FUNDRAISING, NO. 39, SPRING 2003 © WILEY PERIODICALS, INC.

research with professional and volunteer fundraisers highlights both the changing reasons for working with volunteers and volunteers' shifting expectations of fundraising professionals.

In Chapter Two, Donald Zeilstra discusses a new paradigm for considering how professionals can work with and relate to volunteer fundraisers by implementing reciprocal learning in teams. This concept encourages fundraisers not only to teach volunteers about the financial development world but also to be open to learning what volunteers can teach fundraisers about the communities they serve, the business strategies that can be applied in nonprofits, and tactics they may have learned elsewhere.

The volunteer's perspective is presented in Chapter Three by Linda Lysakowski with the question, "What's in it for me?" Her primary research with 104 nonprofit fundraisers indicates that volunteers require more than a pat on the back, but less than what we might think, among other findings.

What prompts an individual to become a fundraiser? I tackle a partial answer to this question in Chapter Four in a preliminary study on relationship building between volunteers and fundraising professionals. This presentation, based on survey results from 140 development officers from across the country, may prove to be controversial and provocative. I welcome readers' feedback and hope to begin a collegial dialogue that will continue for years to come.

We then look more closely at fundraising volunteers in small organizations in Chapter Five through the eyes of Kenneth Knox. Does size matter when considering the volunteer recruitment, training, and management process? Factors beyond size also have impacts on the manner in which volunteers relate to a nonprofit organization. A short case study on the Medical Society Fundraising Network, in which I participate, allows the reader to review and recognize some of the points Knox makes in his work.

In Chapter Six, "The Old College Try: Volunteers in Fundraising Efforts for Small Liberal Arts Colleges," Jody Abzug and Rikki Abzug present an even more narrowly refined view on small nonprofits. Their primary research brings home the points made previously about working with volunteers in small organizations, even ones with strong traditions, centuries of existence, and large professional staffs.

A final case study of the Everybody Wins! Foundation enables the reader to connect the dots from the preceding chapters into one illustrative example in Chapter Seven. Volunteer board president Alan Jones, professional fundraiser Angela Loguercio, and CEO Arthur Makar combine their various perspectives regarding one special event and how it served as a nonhuman change agent for the board and organization. The case presents views from both sides of the table, with some volunteers actively engaged and others content to let the staff lead the charge.

The AFP quarterly research journal is written and edited by volunteers. All of us are involved in fundraising, and we are intimately familiar with the trials and tribulations that the voluntary sector brings to our world. I deeply appreciate the dedication with which each author set about to meet an accelerated deadline for this particular edition. My role in the editing process was a joy.

The mark of a growing profession is the contribution of new knowledge to the information base. By toiling to document, explore, and develop new information for our professional enrichment, these authors and their research subjects have added greatly to the body of knowledge that legitimizes fundraising as a profession.

It is up to you, the reader, to decide if this rise in professionalism in fundraising is in the right or wrong direction, or simply the path of least resistance.

Rebecca E. Hunter
(formerly Fines Fournier)
Editor

REBECCA E. HUNTER (FORMERLY FINES FOURNIER) *is chief development officer for the American Thoracic Society. She has been a fundraiser for twenty-two years in higher education, healthcare, and social services.*

We all want the best possible leadership associated with our organizations. But are the best volunteers available to you? Do you still need volunteers to get the job done? Is a volunteer the best person to make the request for a major gift? What is the model for success?

1

New roles of volunteers in development

Bruce C. Bonnicksen

THE TASK BEFORE ALL AUTHORS of this volume is to explore the nature of volunteerism today and how professional development staff leaders interact with volunteers to advance our institutions. I interviewed sixteen effective volunteers and professional development leaders to gain insight on the topic as it relates to major gift development. These individuals all share a passionate commitment to philanthropy and the nonprofit sector. They have all been involved in the sector for a minimum of fifteen years, some as long as forty years. Some of the individuals will be identified by name and title to lend credibility. However, the majority will be described only by position.

The eight individuals I interviewed whose opinions reflect the views of the donors and volunteers include the following:

Thanks to Sarah Purcell for her research support in the creation of this article.

NEW DIRECTIONS FOR PHILANTHROPIC FUNDRAISING, NO. 39, SPRING 2003 © WILEY PERIODICALS, INC.

- James H. Collins, president of the John Deere Foundation and director of community relations for Deere and Company in Moline, Illinois.
- John Coy, president of The Consulting Network, a firm in Vienna, Virginia, specializing in corporate citizenship, community and employee involvement, and contributions. Among Mr. Coy's clients are Sears, Siemens, Becton Dickinson, Daimler Chrysler, and Charles Schwab.
- Henry W. Holling, vice president and manager of the Caterpillar Foundation, and manager of social responsibility initiatives and corporate public affairs for Caterpillar in Peoria, Illinois.

I also interviewed the chairman and CEO of a regional banking company, a retired and highly successful life insurance agent, the president of a privately held industrial company, and two "professional volunteers and philanthropists."

For confidentiality reasons I will not identify any of the eight persons I interviewed who work in a professional leadership role for various nonprofit organizations. These persons include a woman who serves dual roles as philanthropist and fundraising consultant; two chief executives, one from a small church-related college and the other from a symphony orchestra association (a level-four orchestra out of ten levels); and five chief development officers—three from private universities or colleges, one from a public university, and one from a children's hospital foundation.

In 1985, when I began my career in development, the mantra for success was "volunteer leadership." Having the right volunteers provided the edge for success. With suitable volunteers, campaigns take on an almost elegant feel of ease in the winding path toward the goal. Without effective volunteers, campaigns are a struggle from the beginning.

Most of us understand that successful philanthropy emerges after relationships have been developed with donors and when the case for support meets the giving objectives of the donor. This isn't a simple or short task, but a process that today is more often initiated by volunteers and carried to fruition by staff.

In my development career, I have spent five-and-a-half years in health care, and eleven-and-one-half years in consulting. The trends I have seen in the last ten years point to increased competition for the charitable dollar, a greater reliance on major gifts to achieve goals, fewer volunteers involved in fundraising, and increased use of professional staff for fundraising.

These perceptions were verified in my interviews. For clarity, let me state that all of the persons interviewed, except two, live in small- or medium-sized communities of Iowa, Illinois, and Minnesota. In other words, this chapter reflects the views of Midwesterners in nonurban areas. Trends may be different in other parts of the country or in metropolitan areas.

For the persons I spoke with who represent colleges and universities, staff can and do establish and successfully nurture relationships with major gift donors with little or no involvement by volunteers. For donors to community-based organizations, there remains an expectation that volunteers will ask their peers for major gifts and that the primary relationship with the nonprofit organization is through the volunteer.

However, the role of volunteers is changing. Fewer volunteers are willing to ask for gifts. Competition is fierce to attract the best volunteers—those who have the financial capacity and leadership skills to ask their peers for major gifts. My conversations with volunteers and professional fund-development leaders elicited opinions on volunteering, fundraising, and giving.

Volunteerism is on the rise

Among five of the volunteers I interviewed, there is a general sense of optimism about volunteerism. These persons expressed the strong belief that volunteerism is on the rise in America today, especially in corporations. As volunteer leaders, they make a deliberate effort to encourage and mentor new volunteers. They believe that volunteers can be trained to become effective fundraisers after they have had a good experience with a nonprofit organization. They believe that there are many persons who would volunteer if only they could be identified, given meaningful responsibilities, and mentored.

Volunteering is my work. It adds so much to my life. Finding good volunteers is one of my principal responsibilities, and it can be a challenge. We are in the age of the sound-bite volunteer, 'I'll give you a focused amount of time at some distant point in the future, just don't ask me to come to meetings.'

I can't afford those kinds of volunteers in my organization. Part of my job is reminding myself that being a volunteer is so rewarding. You take someone who's a little shy or reticent about becoming involved and give her a volunteer opportunity where she can make a meaningful impact, and she will blossom. Those volunteers will go the whole nine yards for you. I love my job, especially the part of it that nurtures in others the joy of giving back!

Another volunteer spoke of his optimism about philanthropy and volunteerism.

We have more volunteers in our community than we did ten years ago. More and more people are interested in giving, making larger gifts and planned gifts. We have more nonprofits and a need for more board members. But we have not yet learned how to tap the volunteers available. So many organizations make too little effort to develop and involve people until they really need them for a big campaign. People want to be given a meaningful volunteer role, but they want and need to be asked.

The corporate leaders I spoke with see a relevant and important role for company leaders and employees to be involved in their communities.

We recognize that part of our responsibility as a global company is to be a good community citizen, and in fact there is a strategic reason for doing so. Corporations must show that they are socially responsible. We have an interest in ensuring that the communities in which we have major facilities have ethical, capable, and visionary leaders in the nonprofit sector and in elected public office.

All of our corporate officers serve on at least three boards or have other community involvements. Our expectation is that leaders from our company will apply their personal lessons of success to the organizations they give their time to. We are committed to continually developing leaders for the future. We do that by giving as a company and individually, and by encouraging our people to volunteer and serve on boards. Volunteering rarely just happens; people must be encouraged to get involved and mentored.

Volunteerism is diminishing

Seven persons interviewed expressed an opposite view, that volunteerism—especially among persons age forty and younger—is waning. They are concerned about the future of volunteerism. These persons remember a time as recently as ten years ago when there was a strong sense of responsibility to help others or to improve the community as a volunteer and donor.

Today, these persons see an increasing number of persons under age forty who are looking for some kind of intangible personal benefit in return for serving as a volunteer or making a gift. For example, these donors will make a gift if their children's school will benefit, to demonstrate the success of their business, or because the project will result in community economic growth, benefiting their business.

A philanthropist and retired CEO of a financial services company shared this concern. "I am concerned about the younger generation. They don't seem to have the same sense of responsibility for our community that was cultivated in my generation and previous generations."

The CEO of a regional banking corporation also shares this concern.

Those of us (in this town) who are active in philanthropy and fundraising talk about this all the time. I have friends and business colleagues who are only a few years younger than me who don't give to anything and, of course, don't volunteer. Neither the cause nor how they're asked makes a difference. I've asked them in their offices, at the club, or at a ballgame. They don't have the same sense of responsibility of giving back to the community that I have and my father had.

A university chief development officer commented:

When I began in development in the mid-seventies, the spirit of volunteerism was high. In the eighties, I began to see the emerging professionalism of development and the erosion of the sense of responsibility for community. Unfortunately, more often than not today, philanthropy involves a quid pro quo. And if we are not careful, we will have trained the next generation of leaders to give or volunteer only when they get something in return. The spirit of volunteerism is still there today if you can capture people's imagination. There is a basic altruistic sense about people that if you challenge them they will do it. We have to nurture it.

The data about volunteering and giving portray a positive trend

Despite the difficulties of raising money in the present economy, data from a wide variety of sources suggest that volunteerism and giving is on the rise. Consider these facts:

- The number of 501(c)(3) charitable organizations increased 47.7 percent from 1989 to 1998 (INDEPENDENT SECTOR, 1998).
- From 1991 to 2001, giving after inflation (measured by percent growth in constant dollars) rose 220 percent for community foundations, 146 percent for independent foundations, and 58 percent for corporate foundations (The Foundation Center, 2002).
- The Points of Light Foundation revealed that the number of volunteer centers grew to 470 in 1999 from 416 in 1993. The percent of volunteer centers that manage family volunteering initiatives grew to 44 percent in 1999 from 10.5 percent in 1995 (Points of Light Foundation, 2001).

INDEPENDENT SECTOR (IS) has been conducting a biennial survey on giving and volunteering since 1988. Two clear trends have emerged from the survey series as of the 1999 report (the most recent one that is available at no cost on their Web site). First, volunteers give more than nonvolunteers. In 1998, 47 percent of households both contributed and volunteered. These households gave an average of 2.5 percent of their household income, compared with 1.2 percent among the 23 percent of households that contributed but did not volunteer. Second, as the percentage of volunteers increased, giving rose; and in times of economic recession or uncertainty, giving did not decline as significantly. In each of the survey years, volunteers reported household contributions that were two to four times higher than that for nonvolunteers.

Other relevant findings from the 1999 survey follow:

- Fundraising was the type of volunteer work most frequently performed by 16 percent of survey respondents.
- The percentage of households contributing to charity remained relatively flat from 1987 (71.1 percent) to 1998 (70.1 percent).
- The percentage of households volunteering increased to 55.5 percent in 1998 from 45.3 percent in 1987, the highest-recorded level during the IS survey series.
- Eighty-four percent of all charitable contributions were given by households that also volunteered.
- People who participated as a volunteer during their youth were more likely to volunteer as an adult.
- People are more likely to volunteer when they are asked. In the 1999 survey, 89.5 percent of respondents volunteered when asked.

In 2002, the Consulting Network conducted a national survey of one hundred companies representing more than five million employees. Entitled *Practices in Corporate Employee Involvement Programs*, the data demonstrate that volunteerism is on the rise in corporate America. Among the findings:

- More companies (85 percent in 2002) are offering employee volunteer programs. This is compared to 69 percent of companies responding to the 1997 survey.
- Seventy-nine percent of the participating one hundred companies offer a matching gift program. More than half (fifty-one) of those companies also match employee individual and team volunteerism with a financial contribution.
- An increasing percentage of companies (40 percent in 2002) are expanding their matching program to make more 501(c)(3) organizations eligible.
- Workplace giving programs are conducted in 90 percent of the companies surveyed.
- The majority of those companies that conduct a workplace giving campaign (52 percent) have centralized their campaign, making it companywide, which is up from 47 percent in 1997.
- Forty percent of companies with a workplace giving campaign have broadened their workplace campaigns beyond United Way—an increase from 30 percent in 1997.
- The number of companies offering employees the opportunity to use online giving has grown 94 percent since 1997 (The Consulting Network, 2002).

I could not find any data that measured changes in the percentage of individuals volunteering by age group. The data strongly affirm the value of volunteers as donors and suggests that the spirit of volunteerism remains strong in America. Perhaps if nonprofits can attract and retain volunteers, they can be developed into effective fundraising volunteers.

The role of fundraising volunteers for community-based agencies is changing

My interviews with volunteers and professional development staff revealed how the role of volunteers is changing in fundraising for community-based organizations. The CEO and director of development can solicit a major gift from a prospect who already has a relationship with the organization without the presence of a volunteer. When a major gift prospect does not have a relationship with the organization, a volunteer must be involved, at the very least, to introduce the prospect to the cause. Once an interest has developed, staff can take over the cultivation and solicit the gift. A volunteer can help create interest where none existed previously or elevate the level of the gift to a higher level than the prospect had been considering.

One philanthropist explained:

If it's an organization I'm involved with, then I don't need to be asked for a gift by a volunteer. It's the role of the chief executive to explain the vision for the organization. It's the role of the director of development to ask for my gift and put the request in the broader context of the fundraising strategy. The only time volunteer involvement (in soliciting me) is needed is when I have no relationship with the organization.

The CEO of a family-owned corporation added:

Volunteers used to be involved in campaigns more than they are today. More often than not, the executive director and the director of development call on me, and that's okay. However, if it's an organization I'm not close to and would just as soon ignore, a volunteer can get my attention. A persuasive volunteer can also raise the level of my gift.

The CEO of a children's hospital foundation commented:

Although we are recognized throughout the state as the preeminent health care institution and have instant name recognition, we must have involvement from volunteers in major gift calls. They bring credibility, courage, and community authority. One of our goals is to be in dialogue with two-thirds of our state's hundred most influential leaders by the end of the campaign. We would never get those appointments without volunteer leadership. For this $30 million campaign, we will use less than fifteen volunteers statewide, and they never go alone. Staff always go along to present the case for support and ask for the gift.

Another commented:

I don't mind being asked by a staff member for an annual gift. But I'm offended when a staff member asks me for a large gift on a capital campaign. They usually receive less. Send a board member along with a top staff leader where the volunteer provides the credibility and the staff member makes the pitch.

The corporate leaders interviewed for this chapter measure trust and organizational effectiveness in part by who serves on the board and, in some instances, by who asks. If the volunteer doesn't do the asking, the board is still a critical measure of trust. One corporate leader noted:

We make larger gifts when a board member asks. Nonprofit executives come and go, but the continuity is with the board. We look at who is on the board. If they are people we know, it can affirm the effectiveness of the organization and the validity of the need. Since we're a global corporation, there is no way I could ever know every community, so we look to company leaders in our communities for their insight.

Higher education fundraising is becoming increasingly staff-driven

I believe that all of the development professionals I interviewed would agree with the following statement: "When you have committed volunteers, when they're willing to take and follow through with their assignments, and when they're comfortable asking for gifts, it is always better to have the volunteer make the ask. But, where do I find these leaders, and can I get enough of them involved to make all the calls we need to make?"

All of the fundraisers interviewed represent institutions with a regional or national constituency, and all of them have recently completed or are currently conducting successful capital or endowment campaigns with very little involvement by volunteers. The following statements are direct quotes from different individuals.

Our last capital campaign went over the goal by 10 percent, and we used at most five volunteers.

There is not a history of volunteer involvement in fundraising here. It is completely staff-driven.

I've been doing this a long time, and volunteers today are not as effective as they used to be. I find they don't perform, or there is a reluctance to push for the higher gift. There isn't the same level of commitment to fundraising today that there was years ago.

You have to remember that the cause is what brings staff and volunteers together. The staff are bound to the rules and direction of the institution; the volunteers are not. Therefore, the role of the volunteer must be explicit, even in writing. We have approximately thirty volunteers that we call for help in various capacities. We are selective in who we use and when we use them.

The symphony executive commented:

I used to know three years ahead who my next three board chairs were going to be. I can't say that anymore. It is harder to find committed volunteers. I believe we are moving to a new model of volunteer leadership where much more responsibility is held by staff.

Giving is more personal and strategic

My interviews revealed that there is a new literacy about giving; it has become more personal. Corporate giving is more strategic. Giving to real needs is viewed as a responsibility corporate citizens take seriously. In the past, a volunteer leader with significant influence over a company could exert his or her clout to secure a gift without regard to the cause. Today, more and more companies have specific giving objectives, and grant applicants must meet those criteria.

A corporate foundation executive was adamant in stating that nonprofit organizations must measure their effectiveness:

Nonprofits have to document convincingly that there is a real need for additional services without which the community will suffer. This makes it harder and harder to leverage a gift today.

Another corporate leader said:

Some companies have a discretionary budget set aside within their foundations to use in response to a request from the "right person." The company will make a gift from this budget out of respect for the person who made the request, despite the fact that the purpose of the gift falls outside of the company's giving objectives. These companies still allocate the majority of their giving to causes that meet the company's giving criteria. In other words, they manage the reality of "power fundraising," but still have their strategic giving to address company priorities.

A longtime observer of philanthropy commented:

People are giving to causes they've thought about, know a lot about or are emotionally passionate about. We live in an age where the need is infinite, and information is readily available. There is a sense that giving has become such a personal decision, that to ask for a gift as a volunteer is an intrusion. It is the responsibility of the donor to become informed about and respond to the causes he or she cares about.

A veteran fundraiser said:

That old pitch about how this campaign is good for the community isn't good enough anymore. Organizations have to connect emotionally with their donors or appeal to their interests and values. The solicitor needs to have a thorough understanding of the organization and the case for support to make those connections. The volunteer isn't necessarily the best person to do that.

A vice president of development for a liberal arts college stated:

I never used to hesitate to provide information about a donor's giving history to a volunteer. I would never do that today. My instincts tell me that our donors would view that as a breach of confidentiality. Giving is a personal relationship between our donors and the college.

In this context, the strength of the case for support and the ability to effectively ask for the gift is as important as who asks, as long as the relationships and the credibility have been established.

Roles are shifting in fundraising

I think everyone involved in major gift fundraising understands that securing large gifts is a process of cultivation, asking, following up, and stewardship and that it is a cyclical process. As development professionals, we must understand how to leverage our best volunteers' considerable passion for our mission via their position in the community. One development officer reflected:

I see volunteers having several key roles in fundraising: to identify prospects, to help create an understanding of the cause, to bring credibility by representing the views of the broader community or constituency, and if necessary, to challenge their peers to consider a heightened level of involvement.

What characteristics should we be looking for in identifying potential top volunteers for assistance in major gift fundraising? (1) They are already involved or have been recently; that is, they are well-versed and embrace your mission. (2) There is a personal interest, emotional connection, or a community benefit. (3) There is an opportunity to make a difference.

What are the characteristics of a successful development professional? (1) Help donors emotionally connect to the cause and to continue to remain connected. (2) Help donors see that their support is making an impact. (3) Understand how to measure opportunity, knowing that there are points in the life of the prospect when it is the right time to ask and times when it is not; to be able to match a prospect's level of interest or involvement with the capacity to give. (4) Understand that major gift fundraising is a process and a cycle.

Conclusion

These interviews indicate that volunteer involvement is optional for some organizations. To the extent that we want or need to have volunteer leadership involved in major gift fundraising, development professionals need to look carefully to see the opportunities for new leadership. We must challenge ourselves to creatively recruit new volunteers and immerse them in meaningful causes. Volunteers do not blossom on their own. They must be mentored and helped in their growth as volunteers and donors. This is a joint responsibility of the nonprofit and for-profit community.

I view philanthropy as an American value or certainly a valued tradition, and so do many of the persons I interviewed. Our country was built and made great by people who saw a need that was not being met by government or the for-profit sector and who worked together to meet that need.

Today, our institutions are professionally managed, as they must be. But in doing so, have we eroded the spirit of volunteerism that has been so fundamental to the growth of American society? In my work, I repeatedly find a discouraging lack of knowledge about how the nonprofit sector works. Too many people don't know or have forgotten how America's universities, hospitals, cultural institutions, and human service organizations were established by volunteers. Too many people do not understand that these organizations are actually "owned" by the public good and governed by volunteers. And yet, those institutions make up a vital part of our society.

Try to imagine what our communities would be like without nonprofit organizations. Take your thinking one step further, and try to imagine if no one exercised their freedom to work with like-minded individuals on behalf of a cause that could not be pursued for profit and would not be carried out by government.

During my tenure with a health care organization, I worked for a CEO who, earlier in his career as a practicing attorney, had been part of a group of volunteers that started a free medical clinic. He recounted the story to help me understand that those who recognize the problem are most likely to be the leaders to address it:

Once I understood how serious the problem was (lack of affordable health care) I realized that someone had to do something about it. I kept asking myself, "When were they—meaning the community leaders—going to come up with a solution? When were they going to do something?" Finally I realized that those of us who recognized the problem were "they." We had to start the clinic or no one else would.

The independent data I found in researching this chapter seem to affirm that the spirit of volunteerism is alive and well in America. Perhaps we need to work harder to carve out meaningful roles for volunteers in our organizations. I see opportunity in growing the ranks of volunteers in the nonprofit sector. The long-term benefit will be continuing a tradition that has served America well. And from a myopic or utilitarian perspective, we know that volunteers make the best donors.

Robert Payton posed the belief that philanthropy is "a tradition in jeopardy," in an address presented at a 1998 conference sponsored by the Indiana University Center on Philanthropy called The Future of Philanthropy in a Changing America. In concluding his presentation, Mr. Payton stated:

I am convinced that the philanthropic tradition is in jeopardy, along with tradition in general. Our society is neophiliac, impatient to get on to the next discovery, the next toy. We also seem indifferent to the lessons of the past and largely ignorant of them. What is the old house made of? In the American case: sturdy, durable stuff. . . Who are the stewards of the philanthropic tradition? [Payton, 1998]

I would answer that those of us who practice philanthropy as a profession, as well as the volunteers and donors who work with us, are responsible for continuing the tradition. In other words, there is more to our profession than merely reaching the next goal or earning a good paycheck. We have a responsibility to apply the lessons of this tradition to the changing way philanthropy is being practiced today.

Performance expectations are high in development programs. While volunteer leadership can still be extraordinarily effective without development programs, we must hold high the values of philanthropy.

One top development professional commented, "The more we make this process staff-driven, the more we diminish the gift to a sales transaction. We risk (losing) the spirit of philanthropy."

My challenge to readers: If you are from an organization that needs volunteers to secure major gifts, then those volunteers will be available to you if you get them involved early on, before you ask them to raise money. Find a way to make it happen. If you are from an organization that doesn't need volunteers to raise money, then you have a responsibility to make sure that development is practiced by well-trained professionals who are committed to the ethics of the profession.

I view this chapter as the beginning of a dialogue with readers who want to engage in the discussion. My opinions are shaped by my narrow experience and by my regional exposure to philanthropy. I invite readers to offer their opinions and to further study this question.

References

The Consulting Network. *Practices in Corporate Employee Involvement Programs: Findings from a National Survey.* Vienna: The Consulting Network, 2002.

INDEPENDENT SECTOR. IRS Return Transaction File, 1990–1999, the Urban Institute Center on Nonprofits and Philanthropy. Reported from the *Nonprofit Almanac 1996–1997.* San Francisco: Jossey-Bass, 1998.

The Foundation Center. *Foundation Growth and Giving Estimates 2001 Preview.* New York: The Foundation Center, 2002.

Payton, R. "The Future of Philanthropy in a Changing America." Paper presented at the 1998 Executive Leadership Institute at the Center on Philanthropy at Indiana University, January 1998.

Points of Lights Foundation & Volunteer Center National Network. *Ten Year Review of Accomplishments, 1991-2001.* Washington, D.C.: Points of Lights Foundation & Volunteer Center National Network, 2001. [http://www.pointsoflight.org/research/research.cfm]

BRUCE C. BONNICKSEN *is senior consultant for Braren, Mulder, German Associates, Inc., an Iowa-based fundraising consulting firm established in 1968. The firm presently serves fifty-five small and medium-sized nonprofit organizations including colleges, seminaries, human service agencies, cultural institutions, churches, and civic organizations. Bonnicksen is president of the Quad Cities Chapter of the Association of Fundraising Professionals. He resides in Bettendorf, Iowa, with his wife and son.*

Effective teams—the fundraising professional and the volunteer—develop work practices and access knowledge from one another in a unique way, described as reciprocal learning, that enhances their joint performance.

2

Reciprocal learning in teams

Donald Zeilstra

SECURING THE BEST FROM high-level volunteers in the mission-critical roles of fundraising or governance is a persistent, practical problem for fundraising professionals and managers in the nonprofit sector.

From the colonial period, volunteerism has historically been associated with the work of nonprofit organizations in America, and it continues to be a distinguishing characteristic of the nonprofit sector (Hammack, 1998). Since the early 1900s and accelerating in the post–World War II era, the rise of professionalism in the management of nonprofit organizations was accompanied by university-based nonprofit management centers and the growth of professional associations such as the Association of Fundraising Professionals (AFP).

While the rise of professionalism in fundraising has contributed to wider knowledge of accepted fundraising techniques and improved efficiency of operational management, it may also have the unintended effect of crowding out volunteer leadership, resulting in consequences for the health and vitality of philanthropy and the nonprofit sector. This trend threatens to separate the sector

NEW DIRECTIONS FOR PHILANTHROPIC FUNDRAISING, NO. 39, SPRING 2003 © WILEY PERIODICALS, INC.

from the forces that have characterized it at its best—a focus on altruistic mission, community responsiveness, and accountability that are enhanced by the effective involvement of volunteers.

The rise of professionalism in fundraising is seen in the dramatic increase in the number of paid, full-time development employees in nonprofit organizations, growth in membership and conference participation of professional associations, and growing acceptance of professional certification.

The historic, volunteer-driven, professional staff-supported model of fundraising is espoused in curriculums, professional standards of practice, and the practitioner literature (Pidgeon, 1997), but it is under increasing pressure in practice. Many fundraising professionals report problems of volunteer insubordination—lack of follow-through on assignments or responsibilities, for example—and difficulties in attracting and retaining high-level volunteer leaders for the fundraising campaigns, projects, and efforts that are vital to the ability of many nonprofit organizations' capacity to accomplish their mission. Some scholar-practitioners see the decline of the volunteer-driven model as inevitable (Kelly, 1998).

Simone Joyaux, writing about the fundraising professional's function of enabling volunteer leadership, states, "The not-for-profit sector does not appear to have training programs for enabling. The theory, assets and skills, and strategies or techniques are not found on fundraisers' workshop and conference agendas. It is difficult to find documented models of success or analysis of failure. There is little evidence that professionals gather together to analyze enabling functions, explore assets and skills, and discuss successful and unsuccessful experiences. This must change" (Joyaux, 1994, pp. 31–32).

But in the years since Joyaux's article, there has been little change. Securing the best from high-level volunteers in our fundraising efforts remains an important issue for fundraising professionals.

During the past several years, I have had the opportunity to study the topic of effective utilization of volunteers in fundraising through two exploratory studies of effective professional-volunteer fundraising teams and a current field study using survey research.

Drawing upon recent theory about relational processes and learning in work settings, this chapter presents a conceptual model of effective professional-volunteer fundraising teams.

The main idea is that effective teams—a fundraising professional and a volunteer—develop work practices and access knowledge from one another in a unique way, described as reciprocal learning, that can enhance their joint performance. This chapter proposes that the fundraiser's relationships with a high-level volunteer be taken out of the context of superior-subordinate relationships from which our typical volunteer management practices of solicitation training and volunteer recognition proceed.

Rather, the volunteer-professional relationship can be seen as one of hierarchical equals in which the challenge is to draw upon the knowledge distributed among the team members. Extending situated learning theory to the fundraising context, this chapter presents concepts that emphasize reciprocity in learning—and the associated practices and modes of relationships required for leveraging distributed knowledge.

Organizational studies of volunteers

In recent years, motivation studies on volunteerism have dominated research agendas, yet current trends and problems associated with practice suggest that the useful knowledge produced by these studies is now falling short. Better understanding of the relational processes in volunteering that take into account the knowledge and practices of professional-volunteer fundraising teams promises to provide new insights that may help improve fundraising practice.

Two major case studies of nonprofit organizations conducted in the 1950s looked in depth at volunteers' relationships with professionals. In both cases, the quality of volunteer involvement with the organization was found to affect the level and effectiveness of their participation.

David Sills's analysis of the March of Dimes organization attributes its success in avoiding volunteer apathy, in part, to the fact that chapter volunteers saw themselves as empowered to make decisions and perform the day-to-day tasks of their chapter organizations (Sills, 1957). Chapter volunteers routinely performed tasks that included provision of direct program services, dissemination of information to the public, and private fundraising, tasks that in many nonprofit voluntary organizations are increasingly performed by professional staff.

John Seeley attributed problems in the performance of a federated fundraising organization to latent value conflicts between the different groups of people involved (Seeley and others, 1957). The most prominent group differences were between the professional fundraisers, the lay people who served as volunteer fundraisers, and the professional staff of the organization. These differences were highlighted by the social distance between prominent lay volunteer leaders who came from the business and civic leadership of the community and the professional fundraising practitioners who were closer in attitude and outlook to the program staff of the service-providing affiliated agencies.

Among the dimensions of the latent conflict that Seeley discussed were short-term versus long-term orientation of staff and volunteers, respectively; the degree of pressure to produce results experienced by volunteers and donors; an orientation toward business success or goal attainment on the part of staff versus the maintenance of community relations on the part of volunteers; and democratic versus autocratic orientations toward decision making. Seeley notes that there was no forum for discussion between the different groups where latent conflicts could be brought out, negotiated, and resolved.

The nature of volunteerism is changing along with the demographic characteristics of volunteer leaders. Demographic changes in society have affected volunteerism in ways that underscore the importance of the quality of the professional-volunteer interaction and relationships for securing the best from volunteers.

Historically, volunteer leaders were drawn from the community elite (Smith, 1994). While this element continues to be a very important volunteer leadership resource, today's volunteer leader is more likely to come with significant private-sector experience as entrepreneur, manager, or professional. These volunteer leaders tend to have a greater expectation to contribute their skills and experience and to be involved in planning and policy decision making.

As Barry Karl points out, when volunteers have this level of experience and talent, it raises the question of which member of the team is the professional—the staff manager of the nonprofit organization or the high-level volunteer with significant private-sector or professional experience (Karl, 1998, p. 256).

The position of volunteers in a nonprofit organization has been characterized by structural uncertainty and role ambiguity (Pearce, 1993). Simultaneously, volunteers may be thought of as the "owners" of the organization because they represent the community or constituency, are beneficiaries of the programs and services of the organization, and are also involved in providing these programs and services of the organization through program activities or fundraising.

The introduction of staff complicates the dynamics of the core and peripheral structure that is characteristic of volunteer-driven organizations (Pearce, 1993). It is often unclear which roles are to be played. Do volunteers supervise staff, or does staff supervise volunteers? The answer is uncertain and probably depends on specific situations that may change depending on the task characteristics. However, we know that, within the fundraising context, the relationship between fundraising professionals and volunteers has been characterized as inherently difficult to manage due to role ambiguity and to the multiple asymmetries of status, power, and knowledge (Joyaux, 1994).

The development and recognition model of volunteer management

In recent years, volunteer management has emerged as a distinct professional job category, sometimes with dedicated staff. Standard volunteer management practice has focused on the formal functions of recruitment, training, monitoring, recognition, and evaluation of volunteers (Fisher and Cole, 1993), typically performed by the staff volunteer coordinator. One researcher labeled this approach the "development and recognition" model of volunteer management because it (1) emphasizes training volunteers for development of the specific skills required for performance of their assigned tasks, and (2) recommends the use of recognition as the incentive for performance in the absence of material incentives (Cnaan and Cascio, 1999).

This approach has a strong performance orientation. The emphasis is on the volunteers correctly performing specific tasks and roles. This understanding of volunteer management has become commonplace within the nonprofit sector. The development and recognition model of volunteer management is what most of us do, most of the time, when working with fundraising volunteers.

The development of new theories of relational management (Hoskings, Dachler, and Gergen, 1995; Watson, 2001; Fletcher, 1998) and situated learning (Lave and Wenger, 1991) provide the potential for new and more effective models of professional-volunteer interaction. Past research and practice of volunteer management has been individualistic in orientation, with little sustained focus on relational aspects of the situation or qualities of the professional-volunteer interaction that seem to be so problematic and important for desirable outcomes.

Based on these emerging theories and on my experience as a fundraising professional and consultant, I suggest that the problem of securing the best from volunteer leaders may be better understood in terms of how knowledge is accessed and utilized in the social practices of volunteers and professional staff. From organizational management literature we know that knowledge is an organizational resource that can be managed to affect performance. Although some books on volunteer management have advocated the addition of a reflective learning agenda appropriate for volunteers as adult learners (Ilsley, 1990), the standard model of volunteer management practice has predominantly stressed a performance orientation with need-based, job-specific training for volunteers (Lulewicz, 1995).

However, in addition to the explicit knowledge that can be transmitted as cognitive representations through formal training or captured in databases or manuals, there is a body of social theory that points to the decisive role of tacit or contextual knowledge gained through experience for the ability of individuals to perform in group work settings (Giddens, 1984; Bourdieu, 1977; Garfinkel, 1963). Tacit or contextual knowledge is thought to be particularly important for the spontaneous and strategic decision making required for problem solving, innovation, and the invention of locally appropriate practices and strategies.

Situated learning theory is the primary conceptual resource used here to interpret and understand the expression of knowledge in the social practices of professionals and volunteers (Lave and Wenger, 1991; Lave, 1993).

A situated learning perspective on volunteer management

Jean Lave and Etienne Wenger's (1991) situated learning theory presents a challenge to the standard theory and practice of human resources management that most of us generally employ. Lave's theory holds that it is the qualities and characteristics of the social, relational practices that have the most influence on learning and performance. Formal, performance-oriented methods of volunteer management—such as solicitation training and volunteer recognition—may be a necessary condition for good performance. But on their own they are not sufficient for understanding outstanding effectiveness. In addition, the relational practices must also be analyzed and discussed because this is how the practical knowledge of team members is acquired and expressed.

In situated learning theory, the acquisition and expression of knowledge occurs through the mundane, week-to-week activities of fundraising practice in an ongoing social setting (Lave and Wenger, 1991; Lave, 1993; Wenger, 1998). Because learning is so tightly linked with these everyday social practices, it is frequently occurring in interactions but often is unrecognized by observers or participants.

From the perspective of situated learning, whenever people are interacting, helping each other, or involved together in practical action like fundraising, they have the potential for learning. Whether or not they do learn depends on the qualities of their relationships (Hanks, 1991).

Because individuals are involved in multiple relationships with people having different interests, bases of knowledge, experiences, and social status, there is always the potential for conflict, misunderstanding, and ineffective learning. Relationships that are characterized by frequent interaction, trust, and mutual respect promote a positive learning orientation. On the other hand, inhibited learning relationships are characterized by distance, anxiety, discomfort, and status or power incongruities.

The metaphor of the master and apprentice is used to describe qualities of the relationship in which learning occurs in social settings. Lave and Wenger's (1991) concept of legitimate peripheral participation is central to situated learning theory. It describes the process of a newcomer in the apprentice role, developing into a competent performer of a practice. Through the experience of participating alongside the master in performances that are initially limited but become gradually more realistic and complete, a newcomer acquires the knowledge and skills to be a competent member of the community of the practice.

This insight helps us appreciate the experience of a volunteer in a fundraising effort. Do we provide enough opportunities for limited participation in fundraising? Do we provide opportunities for newcomers to learn from watching more experienced people and then take on more responsibility, or do we expect the newcomer to "sink or swim" in a full-blown fundraising situation with a minimal amount of training?

As useful as this metaphor of master-apprentice relationships is for understanding the experience of volunteers as newcomers, it is inadequate for describing the professional-volunteer relationships common to the fundraising context. The analogy undervalues the distinct knowledge and skills that volunteers bring to the situation. A notable feature of the professional-volunteer fundraising teams I have studied is that the knowledge and skill required for success is distributed between the fundraising professional and the volunteer.

For example, in the fundraising context, each member of the team is both a newcomer and an expert in his or her respective domains of knowledge required for successful fundraising practice (Zeilstra, 2001). Volunteer leaders typically possess greater knowledge of the social networks of the community and skill in framing messages to gain the cooperation of others, often their peers, in that community. This practical knowledge is required for successful fundraising, while the fundraising professionals typically possess greater knowledge and skills in the domain of fundraising techniques, philanthropy, and culture of nonprofit organizations.

To make meaningful the master-apprentice metaphor, one would have to say that each member of the pair was simultaneously in the roles of both master and apprentice in these respective domains. This insight raises a challenge to us as fundraising professionals. How often do we recognize or accept our own role as a learner in our interactions with volunteers? Are we concerned with learning from the volunteers with whom we work? Do we adequately encourage volunteers to express and utilize their knowledge and skills and adopt our own practice accordingly?

The master-apprentice metaphor is also inadequate because it does not account for the complexity of the social setting in which the fundraising professional-volunteer relationship operates. Differences among professionals and high-level volunteers with respect to power and socioeconomic status tend to encourage unequal partnerships that, in turn, hinder performance.

For example, the professional may have expertise in fundraising principles and techniques, but the relationship between professional and high-status individuals who are volunteering may stand in the way of formal methods for training or monitoring practices for performance accountability. Instead of relying on formal management procedures, like meetings and reports, a relational approach to knowledge management in nonprofit organizational settings is suggested. The focus shifts to the qualities and strategy of interaction that professionals adopt, which in turn influences the performance and commitment of the partnership with volunteers.

Do our communication practices, for example, reflect a strongly relational approach? One fundraising professional in the study described her approach for working with volunteer leaders as trying to keep them inspired and reminding them of why they got involved and what a difference they can make, remarking, "If anything, I tend to overcommunicate; I do everything I can to let them know that I am thinking about them."

A key to the process, then, concerns the manner in which the two parties manage their task-based interactions. Their challenge is to create a relationship that enables them to work together in ways that leverage each other's knowledge sets. Understandings of each other's normal ways of functioning would seem to be a key to overcoming this challenge. However, this understanding may be difficult to achieve when the high-level volunteers live and work in different contexts than their nonprofit staff partners.

Further, such understanding may not be necessary. Research on similar challenges in cross-cultural settings indicates that cognitive understanding of each other's ways is not at issue. Rather, effective collaboration that draws on each other's knowledge stems from the two parties jointly developing a set of behavioral interaction practices that works for them (Weisinger and Salipante, 2000). The implication is that the core phenomenon of a reciprocal learning orientation involves the active construction of interaction practices by the actors involved.

In the professional-volunteer relationships common to the fundraising and governance contexts in nonprofit organizations, the professional has the greater opportunity and responsibility for constructing the relationship and practices (Herman and Heimovics, 1990; Joyaux, 1994). The challenge for the professional is to create a relationship characterized by respect and *reciprocity*.

Reciprocity supports the expression of the volunteer leader's community knowledge and leadership skills while at the same time engaging the volunteer in a learning process that provides an opportunity for the volunteer to become increasingly expert in the performance of the practice.

In summary, a situated learning-theory perspective on the fundraising context introduces the concept of reciprocal learning as a contribution to the problem of securing the best from high-level volunteers.

The reciprocal learning model

This section presents reciprocal learning as an alternative model for fundraising professionals to consider in addition to the development and recognition model of standard practice in volunteer management.

The reciprocal learning model proposed for guiding our efforts to secure the best from high-level volunteers is shown in Figure 2.1. It presents the effects of knowledge and practices on outcomes as being mediated or transmitted by how the professional-volunteer fundraising team stands on three traits: performance orientation, learning orientation, and relationship orientation or trust. Each of these concepts is discussed.

Figure 2.1. Conceptual framework of professional-volunteer performance

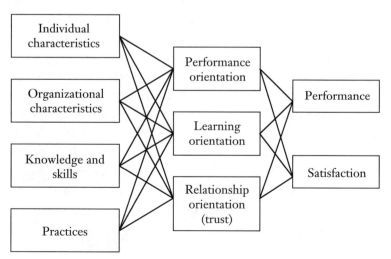

Keep in mind throughout this discussion that the unit of analysis is the professional-volunteer pair. This model is currently being tested through a field study involving survey research.

Performance and learning orientations

A core insight from exploratory research on professional-volunteer fundraising teams is that those who constructed their relationship with the strongest *learning* orientation were more frequently associated with desirable performance outcomes than teams that had *performance* orientation as their dominant trait. Observations of professional behavior that indicated a strong learning orientation included (1) conveying knowledge and skills that the volunteer needs in order to perform his or her role, (2) encouraging the volunteer to use knowledge and skills he or she possesses, (3) jointly developing practices for planning and decision making, and (4) the professional attending to his or her own role as apprentice in learning the knowledge and skills possessed by the volunteer.

Reciprocal learning means that the professional moves beyond exclusively enacting the role of expert that transmits the necessary knowledge/skills, by establishing a relationship in which the learning orientation of both team members is strengthened.

In contrast, observations of behavior indicating performance orientation include reliance on the use of formal training methods for conveying the knowledge and skills that the volunteer needs in order to perform his or her role, and the professional predominantly taking on the role of expert monitoring the performance of the volunteer, instead of enacting joint efforts to do this.

The concepts of performance and learning orientations come from research on how individual goal orientations affect behavior in organizational settings (Button and Mathieu, 1996). The learning orientation concept emphasizes the idea of an individual learning from experience. It matches well with the focus on experiential learning in situated learning theory. If both members of the team are strong in their learning orientation, they will, by definition, be accessing and using the knowledge and skills of their counterpart.

The performance-orientation concept refers to the trait of performing particular tasks in the right way so that they are accomplished without errors. It corresponds with the development and recognition model of volunteer management. The professional is in the expert role, and the volunteer is the novice who needs to learn how to correctly perform the assigned tasks. The performance-orientation concept also includes the idea that a person with a strong performance-goal orientation needs the approval of others for the way the task is done. This fits well with the emphasis on volunteer recognition.

Questions that may help the fundraiser assess how you and your volunteer counterpart stand on these traits include:

- Are you performance oriented? Or learning oriented? Or both?
- Do you strive to provide the tools and skills needed for correct performance of the task?
- Do you focus on the learning process to help newcomers gain the confidence and experience they need in order to be effective in fundraising?
- Do you attend to your own role as learner and try to gain from the experience and social networks of your volunteer counterparts?

Relationship orientation (trust)

Situated learning theory defines learning as changes in attitude, knowledge, or behavior that occur as the result of participation in a social relationship (Lave, 1993). Qualities of the relationship between members of the professional-volunteer fundraising team will affect performance. When members have differential status with respect to knowledge and skills, qualities of the relationship such as respect and trust will facilitate co-participation in developing practices and, consequently, learning. Other qualities of relationships can be detrimental to learning and performance.

For example, Lave and Wenger (1991) describe cases of unproductive learning environments characterized by lack of participation, mistrust, and unresolved power issues. Based on exploratory research and practitioner experience, I believe the important relationship quality for volunteer management is mutual respect, which may be subsumed in a more general concept of trust.

Trust has frequently been used in research as a key variable that differentiates the quality of relationship of two actors in organizational settings (Ganesan, 1994; Sirdeshmukh, Singh, and Sabol, 2002). These researchers have found that interpersonal trust in an organizational setting has three dimensions or components. Breaking it down into these elements helps us understand and apply an often-used concept like trust.

Competence/credibility is the first important dimension of trust. It involves the belief that the other person in the relationship is honest, reliable, knowledgeable, and competent to perform the necessary tasks. This dimension of trust is highly relevant to the knowledge and skills issue of volunteer management that we are highlighting. Distinct domains of knowledge needed in order to attain successful performance are distributed among members of professional-volunteer fundraising teams. Competence needs to be demonstrated in the distinctive domains: for the professional, knowledge of fundraising techniques; for the volunteer, social-network knowledge.

Intention/benevolence is a second dimension of trust. It involves the perception that one party in the relationship intends for the other party to benefit or to profit from the experience. This includes behavior that shows sacrifice, friendship, and other benevolent intentions. In the nonprofit setting, the most important expression of benevolent intention is commitment to the goals and mission of the project demonstrated by behavior that puts the interests of the project above self-interest. One would assume that a benevolent intention would be common in nonprofit settings, but it is important that it is demonstrated by actual behavior in the relationship.

One of the fundraising professionals I studied said, "Relationships are everything, and [they] take time. You have to let people see how you operate and that [you see your role] is more than a job, that you are sincerely interested in the outcomes of this project and what ultimately will be provided for the community."

Problem-solving orientation is the third dimension of trust. It involves an evaluation of the motivation and ability to anticipate and resolve problems. Because performance in this context involves the influence of many decisions and variables that cannot be controlled, there are often many unknowns; each fundraising effort is different. A problem-solving orientation is an important component of trust in this context.

Practical questions for fundraising professionals about the relationship orientation of their teams include:

- How do you rate the trust level of your relationship with volunteers?
- Do you perceive each other as being competent and credible?
- Do you convey your good intentions through actions of going the extra mile for the project?
- Do you recognize and appreciate the sacrifices made by the volunteer on behalf of the project?
- Do you consistently take a problem-solving orientation when challenges or obstacles come up rather than diagnosing faults or assessing blame?
- Are you constantly looking to advance the project and to make adjustments in your working relationship along the way?

The reciprocal learning model suggests that we assess ourselves and our volunteer counterpart on these three orientations. We can be high, low, or medium on each of performance orientation, learning orientation, and relationship orientation. The unique configuration or profile for each of our professional-volunteer fundraising teams will affect the outcome of the work. These configurations represent the concurrent modes of team relationships, and this mode mediates or transmits the effects of knowledge and practice on performance.

A configuration that is high on learning orientation and high on relationship orientation defines the reciprocal learning mode. Configurations that are high on performance orientation and lower on learning orientation and relationship orientation define the development and recognition mode of volunteer management.

Research suggests that the best-performing teams are strong on the reciprocal learning mode because they have a configuration of being high on learning orientation and high on relationship orientation. They are also often high in performance orientation. In contrast, teams that are predominantly performance oriented are high on the development and recognition mode, which is, on its own, less effective in helping teams achieve desirable outcomes.

How knowledge is used by professional-volunteer fundraising teams

How team members access and use their own and their counterpart's knowledge is critical for outstanding performance and securing the best from volunteers. Individually, the members may be strong in some of the knowledge domains that are needed for successful fundraising and less strong in others.

Effective professional-volunteer teams will use the best of each member so that, as a unit, they will be high in many knowledge domains. Comparisons of teams on knowledge domains show different associations with successful outcomes. Teams that leverage the distributed knowledge are strong in many knowledge domains and reach better outcomes. Teams that are less strong overall in the knowledge domains tend to have less desirable outcomes.

A widely accepted and useful definition of the knowledge domains needed for effective fundraising are the six domains that have been developed by the Certified Fund Raising Executive International organization for use in testing for professional certification. These domains were originally developed for certification testing of fundraising professionals with at least five years of experience.

The six domains represent a reasonable and well-considered definition of the knowledge and skills required for a successful fundraising project, a definition that has wide agreement and relevance among fundraising practitioners. Adapting this, the knowledge domains included in the model are: (1) prospect information, (2) donor relationship building, (3) solicitation, (4) volunteer involvement, (5) management, and (6) accountability requirements.

These are presented with representative questions in Table 2.1. It might be useful to review these to help identify the knowledge assets of your fundraising team.

Understanding the distribution of knowledge among the team members is helpful for guiding practice. Based on exploratory research and theory, we expect that the knowledge needed for successful performance is likely to be distributed between the members of the team. How the team members access and utilize this knowledge in the reciprocal learning process is important for performance.

Different patterns of knowledge may be linked to different modes of relationship. If there is a strongly asymmetrical pattern

Table 2.1. Knowledge used by professional-volunteer fundraising teams

To what degree do you and your volunteer counterpart use these knowledge and skills?

Prospect Information
• Identifying people who might support the goals of the fundraising effort
• Identifying "who knows whom" in the community

Relationship Building
• Talking with people in the community to inform them about this fundraising effort
• Educating potential supporters about the benefits of the project

Solicitation
• Asking others for their gifts to support the fundraising effort
• Using the most appropriate solicitation strategies with potential supporters

Volunteer Involvement
• Involving volunteers in the activities of the fundraising effort
• Training volunteers for their work in the fundraising effort
• Encouraging and motivating volunteers to help the fundraising effort

Management
• Managing the people involved in the fundraising effort
• Managing the implementation of the plans for the fundraising effort

Accountability Requirements
• Accounting for the funds raised
• Complying with legal requirements and applicable regulations

with the professional being strong in many domains and the volunteer less strong in many domains, the appropriate training-learning practice is to develop the knowledge and skills of the volunteer. This is consistent with the development and recognition mode.

If the pattern of knowledge distribution is more distinctly distributed by role, the ability to access and use the knowledge requires reciprocity in the relationship, so that the volunteer learns from the professional and the professional learns from the volunteer. This is consistent with the reciprocal learning mode. Research indicates that the volunteer members of effective teams are typically high in the knowledge domains of prospect identification and cultivation, and the professional members are typically high in domains of solicitation and management.

Fundraising professionals who are aware of these patterns can take action to draw out the knowledge and skills of the volunteer so that they can be used in developing strategy and planning action. Spending enough time with volunteers reviewing specific prospective donors and developing the most appropriate solicitation strategies are examples of activities that will have high potential for securing the best from high-level volunteers.

Practices of effective professional-volunteer fundraising teams

The practices of the professional-volunteer team—what they actually accomplish together—have greater effects on performance than do the characteristics of team members or the host organization. The latter factors will be discussed in the next section. Previous research on volunteer management indicates that situational variables, such as the managerial practices that volunteers experienced, have a greater influence on the performance and commitment of volunteers than the personal or demographic variables (Cnaan and Cascio, 1999).

A list of practices that are important for the performance of professional-volunteer teams is presented in Table 2.2. This list was developed from the literature on fundraising and volunteer management and was refined through exploratory research.

Six categories of practices are included: (1) recruitment/enlistment, (2) orientation, (3) training/learning, (4) planning, (5) monitoring, and (6) recognition practices. The practice statements presented in Table 2.2 refer to actions taken or activities performed by the team members. They can be used to assess a professional-volunteer team as a unit. This provides an action-oriented analysis

Table 2.2. Practices of professional-volunteer fundraising teams

To what degree do you and your volunteer counterpart follow each of these practices?

Recruitment/Enlistment
- Volunteers are enlisted by leaders of the project.
- Volunteers are enlisted personally, through a personal appointment or telephone call.
- Volunteers are donors to the organization.

Orientation
- Volunteers are provided a written job description.
- Team members discuss how the project will benefit the community.
- Team members discuss personal goals for their participation.

Training/Learning
- Fundraising training is provided.
- A variety of techniques are used to provide fundraising training.
- There are opportunities to work with more experienced individuals to learn by example.

Planning
- Team members communicate to develop plans for the fundraising effort.
- Team members communicate to assign tasks and responsibilities.
- Team members communicate to develop written materials such as proposals and letters.
- Team members have equal roles in developing meeting plans, setting agendas, and so on.
- Plans are routinely updated and revised based on new information.

Monitoring
- Team members review progress of the fundraising effort.
- Team members solve problems that come up.

Recognition
- Volunteers are informally and formally thanked for their work in the project.
- Volunteers are publicly recognized for their work in the project.

of the relationship to that of team members' knowledge and skills previously discussed.

Research shows that the practices that discriminate most with respect to performance among the teams studied are the extent and variety of methods used in training/learning practices and the frequency of interaction of team members in planning (Zeilstra, 2002). The other categories of practices—enlistment, orientation, monitoring, and recognition—are widely accepted as being important for successful outcomes, but research showed that the amount of variation observed was relatively small. Most of the fundraising professionals studied have similar practices in these areas.

What really made the most effective teams stand out from the others was their emphasis on training and joint planning. These practices have the most potential to secure the best from high-level volunteers and achieve outstanding success.

Because of the significant importance of practices for understanding volunteer management, each category of practices is briefly discussed in this section. The effect of various enlistment or recruitment methods for general volunteers has been studied with mixed and uncertain results. Because fundraising is a high-level organizational activity, like governance, many of the impersonal or mass communication recruitment methods studied in previous research on volunteerism are not particularly relevant for the fundraising context. Instead, social-network recruiting practices in which volunteers are identified from among the constituency of the organization have been found to be the most effective in research and are widely accepted in practice (Cnaan and Cascio, 1999; Dove, 2000).

Orientation for volunteers is recommended by the volunteer management literature. The purpose of orientation is to provide the volunteer with a background and context for making sense of his or her experience and to provide a clear understanding of what is expected. Fundraising professionals should consider practicing all of the following orientation practices in their work with volunteers:

- Discuss on a regular and frequent basis the goals of the project and the benefits for the constituency or community.
- Develop a written job description.
- Discuss the roles and responsibilities of each member of the team.
- Ask about the volunteer's personal goals and objectives for their participation in the project.

The amount and types of training methods are important in discriminating among teams with respect to performance. The better performing cases demonstrate greater frequency and use of multiple methods of training to include formal, informal, and experiential methods.

Formal methods of training, like a group-training event, were practiced to some degree by most of the teams studied and are probably something that most fundraising professionals would do. But do we rely on this alone? The use of multiple methods of training, as well as practices consistent with situated learning theory—such as pairing with more experienced people on fundraising visits—are also important for securing the best from high-level volunteers.

For example, one fundraising professional from a successful team said, "We do hands-on training. We use handouts, a question-answer format, and role plays, and we act out strategies for scheduling and following through on solicitations. As volunteers get better at it, I try not to just repeat it but have them in roles where they are sharing their experience with those less experienced; I often try to send an experienced volunteer out on solicitations with new solicitors so they can see and learn from going along." Modeling appropriate behavior is an accepted and effective adult learning technique.

How are plans and decisions made in your team? Is there frequent interaction in developing project plans or specific solicitation strategies? Do you and your volunteer team member jointly participate in developing meeting agendas or the kinds of documents used in the fundraising effort? Or does the fundraising professional do this alone?

In my research, the teams varied in the frequency and extent of interaction in project planning and problem solving. Teams that were strong on joint planning are associated with better performance.

Monitoring practices involve how team members interact to review progress on tasks and responsibilities. Frequent use of monitoring practices is consistent with a strong performance orientation. Effective teams that are strong in training and planning tend also to be strong in monitoring. What seems to be more of a problem is when monitoring practices dominate the interactions, and other practices are neglected. Monitoring practices can be a sensitive issue. What do fundraising professionals do when things are not going so well—for example, if a volunteer is not following through on an assignment?

One fundraising practitioner of a successful team said, "I try to have a volunteer at a level above the problematic volunteer make a phone call and ask about it, or I do it myself. We have a candid exchange. If they say, 'I've run out of tricks, or out of time,' I ask, 'what can I do to help? Provide more information? Go with you on the call?' I stress that there are a variety of things to do to address the problem."

Recognition is probably the most universally discussed practice in the literature on volunteer management. Similar to donor recognition, recognition of volunteers for their service can be important for building and maintaining motivation of volunteers since there are no real material incentives for their service. Recognition practices should ensure that the volunteer has the personal experience of being thanked and that they are publicly recognized.

Individual characteristics of team members

The management literature indicates that personal characteristics of work team members, including age and gender, affect behavior (Tsui, Egan, and O'Reilly, 1992). In the literature on volunteer research, demographic variables are among the most frequently studied variables for association with recruitment and retention (Wilson, 2000).

In my research on professional-volunteer teams in a fundraising context, the most significant demographic characteristic was experience. Team members' prior fundraising experience can be assessed by years and by the size of the largest they were involved in soliciting, either individually or as part of a team effort.

Experience is important in situated learning theory because it is associated with tacit knowledge. Tacit knowledge built up from experience is a resource that team members draw on to construct interactions with others, to guide practices, and to develop strategies. High levels of tacit knowledge are more effectively mediated to affect performance when there is a strong learning orientation, since in these relationships there is greater opportunity for the team members to express and use their knowledge.

Experience should be assessed independently for both the professional and the volunteer, and jointly for the pair. There are various combinations of experience levels that can characterize a professional-volunteer fundraising team. The best performing teams I studied were those in which both members were high on experience. One might think that experience is an alternative explanation for performance instead of the reciprocal learning mode of relationship. But the teams that had the strongest emphasis on training and learning, using many methods of promoting learning, were those with the most fundraising experience.

One might also expect that the teams with a less experienced member would have a stronger emphasis on training, but this was not the case. The most experienced teams have a better understanding of the importance of pooling their knowledge and thus develop robust training practices. They have experienced how difficult a fundraising effort can be and know firsthand the challenges that arise in such efforts.

Organizational characteristics

Professional-volunteer fundraising teams operate in the context of a larger nonprofit organization. The most significant characteristics that can affect the ability of the team to interact and relate with each other are the size of the organization and the general climate for volunteerism.

First, larger organizations tend to be more established with a larger support base, and this may facilitate fundraising performance independently of the relationship or the practices of the professional-volunteer team.

Second, in larger organizations, a professional-volunteer team may have a proportionally smaller impact on total fundraising performance.

Finally, larger organizations will tend to have larger staffs, and fundraising efforts may tend to be more staff-driven with relatively less significant roles for volunteers. Despite these realities, research and experience suggests that even large organizations can benefit from effective professional-volunteer teams.

If there is conflict or dysfunction within the organization, this can have an independent effect on performance regardless of the relationship or practices of the professional-volunteer team.

For example, in one of the cases studied in my research, tension between executive leadership and the board led to restrictions on the fundraising professional's access to the volunteer, thus hindering the opportunity to develop a relationship. In addition to outright conflict or dysfunction, the literature on volunteer management suggests that the climate or culture of the host organization can encourage or discourage participation by volunteers (Ilsley, 1990).

Performance and satisfaction

Performance and satisfaction are the desired outcomes of the fundraising professional-volunteer team. Ideally, fundraising professionals will want to assess performance by an independent, objective measure, such as the dollar amount of funds raised in a project. But it can be difficult to obtain and compare this kind of data. Performance and satisfaction can also be measured by perceptions of the progress of the project toward the financial goals in keeping with the project's timetable, as assessed by members of the team. Similarly, team members can assess satisfaction about their

Table 2.3. Summary of reciprocal learning model

Individual
Characteristics
• Years of experience
• Largest gift amount

Organizational
Characteristics
• Size
• Climate for volunteers

Knowledge
• Prospect information
• Donor relationships
• Time schedule
• Volunteer involvement
• Management
• Accountability

Practices
• Enlistment/recruitment
• Orientation
• Training
• Planning
• Monitoring
• Recognition

Performance Orientation
• Correct procedures

Learning Orientation
• Abilities; experiences

Relationship Orientation
• Competence/credibility
• Intention/benevolence
• Problem-solving

Performance
• Amount raised
• Solicitation

Satisfaction
• Relationships
• Abilities used

personal role and experience in the project. It is recommended that fundraising professionals regularly discuss team members' perceptions of performance and satisfaction.

A summary diagram of the reciprocal learning model presenting these major concepts and measures is presented in Table 2.3.

Agenda for further analysis and discussion

Ten years ago, Simone Joyaux asked fundraising professionals to discuss and analyze their work with volunteer leaders (Joyaux, 1994). The reciprocal learning model presented here points to a new way of thinking about performance in securing the best from volunteer leaders.[1] The argument here is that topics such as volunteers' motivation and the best practices by which fundraising professionals should manage volunteers have already been the subject of much of our thinking, writing, and practice. It is now a better use of our energy for professional development to pursue new concepts, ones that have been little examined.

The most promising source of new thinking about our practices is that of relational processes and situated learning. The reciprocal learning model provides a promising avenue for continued development of professional practice, one that does not deny the utility of the tried and true development and recognition approaches that we are accustomed to but, instead, offers the hope of identifying and understanding practices that can produce even stronger performance.

Early observational research pointed to particular practices that were learning oriented, and these formed the basis for the development of the reciprocal learning model presented here. More research and practical application is needed to examine learning interactions in professional-volunteer teams—and in larger groupings of people involved in the fundraising context—to better understand the nature of learning processes among volunteers and staff having such different knowledge bases.

The challenge continues to be that of identifying and applying interaction practices that truly differentiate between the successful and less successful development of task-performance knowledge and skill. Current research is taking the results of observational research and subjecting them to quantitative tests, using survey methods to assess variation in the practices that have been discussed in this chapter.

In addition, further work is needed to better understand issues that may affect the nature and effectiveness of reciprocal learning practices. For volunteer leaders in fundraising efforts, a major issue of this type is the impact of status incongruence, with volunteer leaders often having significantly higher socioeconomic status than the fundraising professionals with whom they interact.

We also need to continue to analyze and discuss how reciprocal learning practices may impact volunteer and professional behavior, including volunteer retention, levels of volunteer commitment, volunteers' ability to accept significant responsibility, and staff and volunteer trust in and respect for each other.

Because reciprocal learning practices require higher levels of trust and imply that team members jointly confront performance shortfalls, the relational demands of reciprocal learning are high. The challenges involved in attaining the reciprocal learning mode require us to analyze and discuss factors that may encourage it, including prior fundraising experience, performance and learning orientations, relational dispositions, and differences in social status.

For example, are there types of early interactions between fundraising professionals and volunteers that quickly establish trust and foster or hinder reciprocal learning practices?

Another issue is whether reciprocal learning practices and relationships can be sustained over time. We know that many high-level volunteers believe they have specific skills and knowledge sets to contribute to nonprofit organizations either in fundraising or governance and expect that staff will seek to utilize these. At the same time, staff may have expectations of volunteers as having time and energy too limited to contribute and so may shy away from the reciprocal learning practices described here. Can reciprocal learning practices used in short-term projects carry over to continuing relationships between volunteer leaders and staff?

Conclusion

Advances in the theory and practice of volunteer management can be made beyond currently dominant thought and practice. Implicitly, the reciprocal learning model of volunteer management proposes that the relationship of high-level volunteers with fundraising professionals must be taken out of the context of superior-subordinate relationships from which standard volunteer resource management concepts of development and recognition proceed.

Rather, the volunteer-professional relationship can be seen as one of knowledge and hierarchical equals in which the challenge is to draw upon the knowledge distributed between the team members. By extending situated learning theory to this particular relational context, I have presented concepts that emphasize reciprocity in learning as well as the associated practices and modes of relationships required for leveraging distributed knowledge. The results of current research and continued analysis and discussion may provide practical guidance for fundraising professionals concerned about securing the best from volunteer leaders involved in fundraising and other mission-critical activities of nonprofit organizations.

Note

1. The author would like to thank Paul Salipante for his contributions to the ideas in this chapter, particularly those discussed in this section.

References

Bourdieu, P. *Outline of a Theory of Practice*. Cambridge, U.K.: Cambridge University Press, 1977.

Button, S. B., and Mathieu, J. E. "Goal Orientation in Organizational Research: A Conceptual and Empirical Foundation." *Organizational Behavior and Human Decision Processes*, 1996, *67*(1), 26–48.

Cnaan, R. A., and Cascio, T. A. "Performance and Commitment: Issues in Management of Volunteers in Human Service Organizations." *Journal of Social Service Research*, 1999, *24*(3/4), 1–37.

Dove, K. E. *Conducting a Successful Capital Campaign*. San Francisco: Jossey-Bass, 2000.

Fisher, J., and Cole, K. *Leadership and Management of Volunteer Programs: A Guide for Volunteer Administrators*. San Francisco: Jossey-Bass, 1993.

Fletcher, J. K. "Relational Practice: A Feminist Reconstruction of Work." *Journal of Management Inquiry*, 1998, *7*(2), 163–186.

Ganesan, S. "Determinants of Long-Term Orientation in Buyer-Seller Relationships." *Journal of Marketing*, 1994, *58*(2), 1–19.

Garfinkel, H. "A Conception of, and Experiments with, Trust as a Condition of Stable Concerted Actions." In O. J. Harvey (ed.), *Motivation and Social Interaction*. New York: Ronald Press, 1963.

Giddens, A. *The Constitution of Society: Outlines of the Theory of Structuration*. Berkeley: University of California Press, 1984.

Hammack, D. C. (ed.). *Making the Nonprofit Sector in the United States*. Bloomington and Indianapolis: Indiana University Press, 1998.

Hanks, H. "Foreword." In J. Lave and E. Wenger (eds.), *Situated Learning: Legitimate Peripheral Participation*. Cambridge, U.K.: Cambridge University Press, 1991.

Herman, R. D., and Heimovics, R. D. "The Effective Nonprofit Executive: Leader of the Board." *Nonprofit Management and Leadership*, 1990, *1*(2), 167–180.

Hosking, D. M., Dachler, H. P., and Gergen, K. J. *Management and Organization: Relational Alternatives to Individualism.* Aldershot, U.K.: Avebury, 1995.

Ilsley, P. J. *Enhancing the Volunteer Experience: New Insights on Strengthening Volunteer Participation, Learning and Commitment.* San Francisco: Jossey-Bass, 1990.

Joyaux, S. P. "Voluntary Association and Volunteer Leadership." *New Directions for Philanthropic Fundraising*, 1994, *5*, 17–32.

Karl, B. D. "Volunteers and Professionals: Many Histories, Many Meanings." In W. W. Powell and E. S. Clemens (eds.), *Private Action and the Public Good*, New Haven, Conn.: Yale University Press, 1998.

Kelly, K. *Effective Fund-Raising Management.* Mahway, N.J.: Erlbaum, 1998.

Lave, J. "The Practice of Learning." In S. Chaiklin and J. Lave (eds.), *Understanding Practice: Perspectives on Activity and Context.* Cambridge, U.K.: Cambridge University Press, 1993.

Lave, J., and Wenger, E. *Situated Learning: Legitimate Peripheral Participation.* Cambridge, U.K.: Cambridge University Press, 1991.

Lulewicz, S. "Training and Development of Volunteers." In T. Connors (ed.), *The Volunteer Management Handbook.* New York: Wiley, 1995.

Pearce, J. L. *Volunteers: The Organizational Behavior of Unpaid Workers.* London and New York: Routledge, 1993.

Pidgeon, W. P. "Volunteer Led Solicitations." In J. M. Greenfield (ed.), *The Nonprofit Handbook: Fundraising.* New York: Wiley, 1997.

Seeley, J. R., and others. *Community Chest: A Case Study in Philanthropy.* Toronto: University of Toronto Press, 1957.

Sills, D. L. *The Volunteers: Means and Ends in a National Organization.* Glencoe, Ill.: Free Press, 1957.

Sirdeshmukh, D., Singh, J., and Sabol, B. "Consumer Trust, Value, and Loyalty in Relational Exchanges." *Journal of Marketing*, 2002, *66*(1), 15–37.

Smith, D. H. "Determinants of Voluntary Association Participation and Volunteering: A Literature Review." *Nonprofit and Voluntary Sector Quarterly*, 1994, *23*(3), 243–263.

Tsui, A. S., Egan, T. D. and O'Reilly, C. A. "Being Different: Relational Demography and Organizational Attachment." *Administrative Science Quarterly*, 1992, *37*(4), 549–580.

Watson, T. J. *Organizing and Managing Work: Organizational, Managerial, and Strategic Behavior in Theory and Practice.* Upper Saddle River, N.J.: Prentice Hall, 2001.

Weisinger, J. Y., and Salipante, P. F. "Cultural Knowing as Practicing: Extending Our Conceptions of Culture." *Journal of Management Inquiry*, 2000, *9*(4), 376–390.

Wenger, E. *Communities of Practice: Learning, Meaning, and Identity.* Cambridge, U.K.: Cambridge University Press, 1998.

Wilson, J. "Volunteering." *Annual Review of Sociology*, 2000, *26*(26), 215–240.

Zeilstra, D. "Learning Together: Practitioner/Volunteer Interactions in Effective Communities of Practice." Paper presented at the Association for Research of Nonprofit Organizations and Voluntary Associations Conference, Dec. 1, 2001.

Zeilstra, D. "Performance and Commitment of Professional-Volunteer Partnerships." Paper presented at the Association for Research of Nonprofit Organizations and Voluntary Associations Conference, Nov. 13, 2002.

DONALD ZEILSTRA *is senior consultant and staff supervisor for Ketchum, and a Mandel Center for Nonprofit Organizations/Executive Doctor of Management Fellow at Case Western Reserve University.*

Almost all nonprofit organizations seek volunteers to help with their fundraising efforts. Often they are stymied by their inability to recruit and retain effective volunteers. Examining this situation from two views—the volunteers' perspective and that of organizations successful at retaining active volunteer fundraisers—may help struggling organizations chart a path to success.

3

What's in it for me?

Linda Lysakowski

PREVIOUS CHAPTERS NOTE that volunteers' reasons for giving time and money to nonprofits have changed from generation to generation. Altruism often gives way to a quid pro quo attitude. What are their strategies to address this paradigm?

What do volunteers look for in institutions?

In *The Seven Faces of Philanthropy* (1995), Russ Alan Prince and Karen Maru File talk about seven types of people and what motivates each to give: Altruist, Communitarian, Devout, Investor, Socialite, Repayer, and Dynast.

In his book *Megagifts* (1984), Jerold Panas remarks that donors give for many different reasons, but above all is the belief in the organization's mission.

NEW DIRECTIONS FOR PHILANTHROPIC FUNDRAISING, NO. 39, SPRING 2003 © WILEY PERIODICALS, INC.

Like donors, volunteers become involved for many reasons, including family history, religious influence, altruism, wanting to give back, community spirit, investing in their own or someone else's future, or because it is fun. But if they do not believe in the mission of the organization, they will not be effective volunteers who can successfully ask a potential donor to contribute to the organization.

Methodology

A recent survey, conducted as primary research for this chapter among 104 nonprofit fundraisers, shows by a 2 to 1 margin that "belief in the mission of the organization" outnumbers all other reasons listed for retaining fundraising volunteers. In-depth interviews with eight volunteer fundraisers confirmed these findings.

Survey of nonprofits

Nonprofits that use volunteers fundraisers

Yes	88
No	16
Total Nonprofits Surveyed	104

Who recruits volunteer fundraisers and how they recruit them

Board	76
Staff	67
Other volunteers	67
Users of organization's services	5
Community contacts	4
Newsletters	2
Volunteer center	2
Americorp	1
Posters, PSAs	1

Support provided for volunteer fundraisers

Volunteer packets/materials	52
Joint calls with staff and board	49

Volunteer orientation	46
Formal volunteer training	28
Individual coaching/mentoring/ encouragement	11
Staff support	6

Length of volunteer fundraisers' involvement with organization

Less than one year	14
One to two years	17
Three to five years	25
Six to nine years	9
More than nine years	7

Types of recognition given to volunteer fundraisers

Recognition gifts	44
Recognition events	41
Personal letters and cards of thanks	18
Publications of organization	14
Verbal thanks	7
Recognition at events other than specific recognition events	7
Certificates	4
Newspaper ads	2
Nominations for national awards	1
Promotion to further involvement	1

Reasons cited for ability to attract and retain volunteer fundraisers

Belief in mission of organization	26
Recognition and appreciation	14
Personal relationship with staff	9
Staff support	9
Knowing they make a difference	8
Peer recruitment	7
Training	5
Meaningful work	4
Communication	3

Listening to their ideas	3
Matching volunteer interests with organization's needs	3
Organization and planning	3
Quality of board	3
Success in fundraising	3
Flexibility	2
Keeping tasks short term	2
Keeping volunteers involved	2
Orientation	2
Strong development committee	2
Taking the fear out of fundraising	2
Accountability	1
Credibility	1
Giving volunteers specific tasks	1
Grateful service recipients	1
Mutual respect	1
Team solicitations	1
Treating volunteers like good employees	1
Willingness to make a financial commitment	1

Survey of volunteers

Number of organizations volunteered for

One	1
Two to five	6
More than six	1

Recognition preferred by volunteers

Personal letter or card	4
Printed list of volunteers in newsletter or other organization publications	2
Recognition event	2
No recognition	2
Phone call	1
Recognition gift	1

Expectations of organizations for which they volunteer

Staff support	5
Materials and information	5
Well-prepared staff	1
Meaningful work	1
Clear instructions	1
Timely response	1
Appreciation	1

Alicia P. von Lossberg of the South Carolina Tennis Association reports that many of her volunteers "are passionate about the value of tennis in the physical well-being of participants and feel that [it] is a character building game for (young people) to take through life." Alicia feels her volunteers want to identify with her organization, want recognition, and have the time to devote to attain the goals established by her organization.

Likewise, Bob Crandall of American Baptist Churches USA (Valley Forge, Pennsylvania) says his "cause is appealing . . . they want to help us succeed." Almost all nonprofit organizations do fundraising. Some are dependent on volunteers because they have little or no development staff or because staff do not have the expertise to ask for money. Others believe that recruiting volunteers to help in their fundraising effort is the most effective way to get the job done. Most practice the theory that a peer-to-peer request is almost always the most successful. Usually the nonprofit fundraising staff person, and sometimes even the CEO, is not a peer of the major donors they are soliciting. Volunteers are not being paid to fundraise as staff is. Therefore, volunteers bring something special and unique to the table that staff cannot provide when meeting with a prospective donor.

Why do some organizations excel at recruiting and retaining volunteer fundraisers?

Volunteers are recruited in various ways by nonprofits. Sometimes the development director, executive director, or other senior staff member is the person who recruits the fundraising volunteers; board members or other volunteers recruit the remainder.

Lori Oziri of the Reading-Berks Emergency Shelter (Reading, Pennsylvania) says her staff are passionate about their mission, and that fact helps them recruit volunteers because volunteers see that passion. Sometimes volunteers are approached through a corporate volunteer program, a volunteer center, or program such as the Leadership Program.

The aforementioned survey illustrates that sometimes an organization's end users or clients help recruit volunteers. A few volunteers may actually volunteer without being asked because they know of an organization's good works and want to help raise money to continue or expand its programs and services. The most effective way to recruit is usually for a well-respected person to ask others to volunteer, similar to peer-to-peer solicitation.

James Brogna of Allied Services Health System (Scranton, Pennsylvania) says, "Quite possibly, having the right person ask (a volunteer) to help is the biggest factor in our recruiting volunteer fundraisers."

United Way is a classic example of a volunteer-driven fundraising effort. Says Ted Flaum of the United Way of Southern Nevada (Las Vegas, Nevada), "I hardly ever make an ask of a major donor myself. My role is to work with the volunteer fundraisers, to strategize about who is the best asker, what is the right amount and the right project for which to solicit this prospect."

Volunteers for United Way campaigns are generally recruited through their workplace and often are given paid time by their employers to serve as loaned executives for United Way. Other nonprofits may be equally successful at recruiting fundraising volunteers. Some are very clear about making fundraising a requirement of serving on the board.

Hospitals, colleges, and universities typically have a larger development staff than smaller organizations such as human services agencies, arts groups, and environmental organizations. Yet higher education and health care often excel at utilizing volunteers in their fundraising efforts, indicating that staff size does not always determine whether volunteers are used.

Many college annual campaigns use dozens, if not hundreds, of volunteers to accomplish their fundraising goals. Capital campaigns are very volunteer-intensive. An organization that has not used volunteers effectively in its annual fundraising efforts may experience difficulty in recruiting volunteers to implement a successful capital campaign. Nonprofits are advised to place more emphasis on volunteer fundraising, along with recruitment of board members and other volunteers who can help implement this process.

Joan Priest at the Delaware Nature Society (Hockessin, Delaware) says:

Leadership is key for us. Starting at the top—getting the wonderful worker that will lead the team, the one person that no one can refuse—is a surefire way to succeed. Just like fundraising, it's the right person asking them at the right time to do the right task.

We usually use the president and the executive director to recruit that leader, and we spend a lot of time and effort up front. Once the leadership is in place, we give that person and his or her committee everything we can to make their job easier. We try to make sure that they succeed in their first calls, and that their experience is a positive and reinforcing one, so that we are all happy and feel rewarded in our effort. We are always training new volunteers on the annual giving and special-event committees, but we also have some amazing leaders who have stayed with us through thick and thin.

What motivates volunteers to get involved in an organization's fundraising efforts? For many board members, it is seen as an obligation to ensure the fiscal stability of the organizations. Volunteers report that they are willing to do fundraising for those nonprofits that have a mission or cause in which they believe but also that give them the support volunteers need, including staff communication and information. Recognition gifts do not seem to excite volunteers, but a simple thank you, a published acknowledgment, or perhaps a fun recognition event is what they are looking for, according to the volunteers surveyed.

For many organizations' staff, the use of volunteers to help with their fundraising is just something they have never considered. Staff may not feel comfortable asking for money and can not imagine why a volunteer would feel any differently.

Other organizations may feel they have the internal skills to do fundraising, or it may just be easier to do it themselves rather than recruit, train, and support volunteers.

Senior management or board members often have the attitude, "That's why we hired the fundraiser, so we don't have to do it." (How many times have we heard that?!!!)

A number of organizations in the survey mentioned that they are new start-up groups and plan to implement the use of volunteers in their fundraising efforts, but that they simply have not had time to start a volunteer recruitment program. These organizations may be missing some of the biggest opportunities of their organizational lives: the chance to actively engage volunteers who can speak effectively and passionately about their organization from a uniquely special perspective; the option to grow their fundraising programs by involving more individuals; and the likelihood of identifying effective volunteers who can become great board members.

Is a good fundraiser born, or is fundraising an acquired skill?

Professional fundraisers often joke about the fact that no one sets out as a child to be a fundraiser when they grow up. Very few of us seem to be "born to raise," although good fundraisers do seem to share some common traits. Panas (1988) lists qualities to look for in a professional fundraiser. The top five are (1) impeccable integrity, (2) good listener, (3) ability to motivate, (4) hard worker, and (5) concern for people.

These same qualities should be sought in volunteer fundraisers as well. Fundraising can be taught or learned from experience. Today there are courses for professional fundraisers available online and on college campuses throughout North America. While most of the participants in fundraising conferences, workshops, and formal education classes are professionals pursuing it as a career, some volunteers will gladly avail themselves of this training in order to better help the organizations they care about.

Cheryl Ghirlando, a volunteer for her children's preschool in Las Vegas, Nevada, currently attends a ten-month training program at her own expense in order to better help her organization with its fundraising efforts. When the Association of Fundraising Professionals' international conference was held in Philadelphia a few years ago, one consultant met a married couple that had flown there from Phoenix, again at their own expense, because of the wife's involvement on the boards of several nonprofits.

How can an organization better prepare its volunteers for fundraising?

Orientation: Many of the organizations surveyed replied that they had an orientation program for volunteer fundraisers. Volunteers can gain a good foundation for speaking to others about the organization when given a tour of facilities and shown a video or PowerPoint presentation explaining the mission, history, and programs of the organization. Adult learners need to be presented information in a variety of formats—printed, spoken, visual, and auditory—because different people learn in different ways.

To help volunteers overcome the "fear of fundraising," strategize with them to identify the best solicitors for team visits. A technique used by many organizations is to involve staff or a board member of the organization.

Robbe Healey of The Hickman (West Chester, Pennsylvania) adds, "The culture (of volunteers) is changing—people being recruited realize the impact a well-conceived and well-executed philanthropy program can have, and are willing and eager to be change agents."

Training: Few organizations in the survey responded that they have a formal training program. However, a greater number provide background material in the form of a volunteer training packet or manual.

Staff, consultants, and other volunteers can conduct formal training programs. One successful model involves bringing in well-respected volunteers from a nonprofit organization with a successful fundraising program, to talk to the board about their fundraising responsibilities.

During training, it is essential to educate volunteers regarding the impact of their role on the organization and the community. Charles Nagle of the Institute of Notre Dame (Baltimore, Maryland) says that letting his volunteers know they "make an impact" in any success his organization has and getting to know the volunteer before the "ask," along with making them feel important and recognized, are the keys to his success with volunteer fundraisers.

On the other hand, a different professional fundraiser said that their organization has no problem attracting volunteers who believe in their mission, but because they have not done a particularly good job nurturing or training their volunteers, volunteers lose interest after their initial fundraising forays.

A third organization reported that in the past, volunteer training sadly had not been a top priority for her organization, but now they are emphasizing training. Yet a fourth reports they have not done a good job of designing a program to keep volunteers involved over the long haul.

Support: Staff support is crucial to the success of a volunteer. A number of organizations in our survey provide one-on-one mentoring, coaching, and support for the volunteers once they begin their fundraising tasks. One professional fundraiser remarks that the office support provided to volunteers, plus a *lot* (speaker's emphasis) of praise, is what keeps her volunteers motivated and coming back for more.

Katie O'Neill-Herrington of the Susan P. Byrnes Health Education Center (York, Pennsylvania), commented, "We have made the process easy for them. Letters are generated by staff, stamps are already stuck on the envelopes, so 'all' they need to do is sign their name and make follow-up phone calls."

Involvement: Joe Scialabba of the Roman Catholic Diocese of Altoona-Johnstown (Holidaysburg, Pennsylvania) suggests that listening to the ideas of volunteers and implementing change based on these ideas helps him retain good volunteers. Long-term relationships are often started with a short-term assignment: serving on an annual appeal drive, a capital campaign, or a special event can often lead to a long-term relationship.

Some organizations reward their volunteers by elevating them to a higher level, including the possibility of board membership.

Phyllis Spencer Miller of the Council on Drug and Alcohol Abuse (Lancaster, Pennsylvania) adds that her personal involvement with volunteers is the single biggest factor of her success in retaining volunteers. "I take the time to get to know them and keep in touch throughout the year. I don't just 'love them and leave them.'"

Giving volunteers specific tasks and matching the tasks to the person is also important. There are many ways a volunteer can help with the organization's fundraising efforts: making the request for a major gift, helping at a phonathon, writing appeal letters, planning and working at events, making thank you calls or writing thank you letters to donors, and identifying and cultivating potential donors.

Communication: Phone calls, e-mail and other ways of staying in touch with volunteers are crucial. As Judy Dickinson of Interfaith Housing Services, Inc. (Hutchinson, Kansas) says, "They need to be made to feel as important as they are! Never take them for granted! Listening to what they want to do to help is important too. They won't stick around if they don't like what they are doing."

Betsy Gerdeman of WETA TV (Alexandria, Virginia) adds, "Going over the top in communicating to them how important their efforts at fundraising are to the organization and how greatly appreciated they are for what they do" makes all the difference.

Recognition: While there are many ways to recognize volunteers, most volunteers feel that a simple thank you letter or card, or a personal phone call or word of thanks, is the most appreciated. As Verla Custer of Girl Scouts—Irish Hills Council (Jackson, Mississippi) notes, the key is "recognition, recognition, recognition; thank you, thank you, thank you."

Volunteers say they are successful in raising money for organizations that have a clearly defined mission in which they feel involved and committed. The organization must make good use of their time and talents. They need support from the organization. An organization that provides adequate training and support for their volunteers will be more successful in recruiting and retaining good volunteers.

References

Panas, J. *Megagifts*. Chicago: Pluribus Press, 1984.
Panas, J. *Born to Raise*. Chicago: Pluribus Press, 1988.
Prince, R. A., and Maru File, K. *The Seven Faces of Philanthropy*. San Francisco: Jossey-Bass, 1995.

LINDA LYSAKOWSKI *is president and CEO of CAPITAL VENTURE^SM, a fundraising consulting firm with offices in Nevada, Pennsylvania, and Florida. One of only seventy people worldwide to hold the Advanced Certified Fund Raising Executive (ACFRE) designation, Linda is a graduate of AFP's Faculty Training Academy and a frequent presenter at international and regional conferences. She has been published in CASE Currents and the International Journal of Nonprofit and Voluntary Sector Marketing, among others.*

Is the adult child of an alcoholic more adept at building relationships because of his or her experiences in navigating and surviving an alcoholic family, and more prevalent in this profession than in the general U.S. population? If so, for what reasons?

4

Relationship building between volunteers and fundraising professionals: Does the adult child of an alcoholic prevail in our profession? A preliminary study

Rebecca E. Hunter (formerly Fines Fournier)

FUNDRAISING IS A COMBINATION of science and art. The science part includes the technical information and functional responsibilities that are learned by doing. The art is less quantifiable. A major factor in the art of fundraising is building relationships. This chapter examines the hypothesis that the adult child of an alcoholic (ACoA) (see Exhibit 4.1 for definition and characteristics) is more adept at building relationships and more prevalent in the field of fundraising than in the general U.S. population.

Many thanks to those who shall remain anonymous for their personal contributions to this chapter.

NEW DIRECTIONS FOR PHILANTHROPIC FUNDRAISING, NO. 39, SPRING 2003 © WILEY PERIODICALS, INC.

Exhibit 4.1. Definitions and characteristics of ACoAs and codependency

What Is an Adult Child of an Alcoholic?

Various groups use different abbreviations for this recognized social disorder: ACA, ACoA, TOVA (The Other Victims of Alcoholism), COSA (Children of Substance Abusers), COA (Children of Alcoholics).

Regardless of the label, the ACoA can be a survivor. Those who survive are strong individuals who, as children, coped with a "home" (a loosely applied term) defined by chaos, trauma, confusion, embarrassment, lies, and pain. As adults, ACoA's carry the scars of growing up in this dysfunctional environment.

Professionally, an ACoA is often likeable, caring, responsible, successful, and easygoing. Because we've become so good at denial, taking on too much, and trying to please everyone all of the time, we often appear to be able to handle anything.

Commonly accepted ACoA characteristics include some of the following:

- Is confused about what "normal" is.
- Feels inherently different from others.
- Lies when telling the truth would be just as easy.
- Feels guilty when standing up for self, and gives in to others instead of taking care of self.
- Denies, minimizes, or represses feelings from traumatic childhoods, and has difficulty expressing feelings.
- Has difficulty relaxing and having fun.
- Takes self very seriously.
- Has trouble with intimate relationships, lacks trust in others, feels insecure, and is unable to define clear boundaries.
- Habitually chooses relationships with emotionally unavailable people, even those from whom we solicit gifts.
- Tends to self-isolate and feels uneasy around others, especially authority figures.
- Is a dependent personality who is terrified of rejection or abandonment, and stays in jobs that are harmful because of feeling hopeless and helpless.
- Has a strong need to be in control and overreacts to change that cannot be controlled.
- Tends to be impulsive and takes action before considering alternative behaviors or possible consequences.
- Acts either super-responsible or super-irresponsible.

Exhibit 4.1. *(continued)*

- Is intimidated by angry people and personal criticism, creating anxiety and over sensitivity.

What Does It Mean to Be Codependent?

Codependents share many behaviors with ACoA's, and an ACoA who is not in recovery is likely codependent in his or her relationships, both at work and at home. A person will always be an ACoA; it is possible to break free from codependency by unlearning and replacing codependent behavior.

Additional significant traits of a codependent person include (Hemfelt, Minirth, and Meier, 1989):

- Driven by one or more compulsions
- Bound and often tormented by the way things were in the dysfunctional family of origin
- Frequently maturity is very low
- Certain his or her happiness hinges on others
- Relationships are marred by a damaging, unstable lack of balance between dependence and independence
- Master of denial and repression
- Life is punctuated by extremes
- Constantly looking for the "something" that is missing or lacking in life

A joke circulating in the codependent recovery community is about four codependent drivers, each sitting in his or her own car at a four-way stop sign. Traffic was at a standstill because each one kept motioning for the other driver to go ahead, a classic illustration of denial of one's own needs, putting other people's happiness first, literally driven by the compulsion to please someone else!

Statistics

The Children of Alcoholics Foundation (COAF) states that one out of every eight Americans is raised in an alcoholic home. This means that 12.5 percent of the population is an ACoA. In 1988, it was estimated that 28 million Americans are ACoA and still exhibit the codependency they experienced in their childhood (Hemfelt, Minirth, and Meier, 1989).

The *American Journal of Public Health* (2000) places that rate even higher. Using data from the 1992 National Longitudinal Alcohol Epidemiological Survey, authors from the National Institute for Alcohol Abuse and Alcoholism (NIAAA) determined that approximately one in four children in the United States is exposed to alcohol abuse or dependence in the family at some point before age eighteen. This would place the ACoA rate at 25 percent of the general adult population.

Methodology

A voluntary, random selection survey was conducted in St. Louis at the 2002 Association of Fundraising Professionals' (AFP) International Conference, during which 140 attendees completed 26 true-false statements. The survey was referred to as a "professional career selection questionnaire." Every "true" response indicated a behavior exhibited by ACoAs. (See Exhibit 4.2 for a copy of the survey.)

To disprove this hypothesis, up to 25 percent of the respondents could qualify as ACoAs and still not exhibit a larger presence in the fundraising population than in the general population.

Why not ask directly if the respondent is an adult child of an alcoholic? Asking such a blunt question and obtaining an honest answer would be difficult for several reasons. (1) Shame is a hallmark trait of someone growing up in an alcoholic household. (2) Denial is also a leftover condition from the family dynamic. (3) Many people may not recognize themselves as an ACoA. (4) Even if an individual is familiar with the phrase and recognizes him- or herself as such, he or she may not be comfortable with the term applied personally.

This survey was reviewed and approved by Barbara Benton, M.D., board certified in psychiatry. Statements were drawn from research findings presented in several standard mass-market ACoA publications (Beattie, 1992; Burnett, 2002; Friends in Recovery, 1996; Krisberg, 1998; Woititz, 1989). Respondents were told that this survey was to "help test a hypothesis regarding the types of people who are drawn to, and therefore may be better than average at, fundraising as a career."

Exhibit 4.2. Survey Instrument, AFP 2002 International Conference

Thank you for agreeing to complete this professional career selection questionnaire. A random sampling will help test a hypothesis regarding the types of people who are drawn to, and therefore may be better than average at, fundraising as a career. This survey should take no more than five minutes to complete. All responses are completely confidential.

Consider these statements in relationship to those in your work world, including colleagues, staff, supervisors, volunteers, prospects, and donors.

True	False	
T	F	I am very sensitive and responsive to the needs of other people.
T	F	I often feel responsible for the happiness and well-being of others.
T	F	People look to me in the midst of a crisis.
T	F	Friends would describe me as a perfectionist.
T	F	It's hard for me to recognize my own accomplishments.
T	F	Criticism is difficult for me to accept, even when constructive.
T	F	People ask me for help because they know it's hard for me to say no.
T	F	I constantly seek approval and affirmation.
T	F	I have trouble relating to authority figures and angry people.
		While growing up, I would describe myself as (check all that apply):
T	F	a Caretaker
T	F	b Clown
T	F	c Overachiever
T	F	d Underachiever
T	F	When things seem to be going too well, I'm always waiting for the other shoe to drop.
T	F	Sometimes I feel guilty when I stand up for myself instead of giving in to the wants and needs of others.
T	F	I judge myself more harshly than I judge other people.
T	F	I take myself too seriously.
T	F	I would consider myself a successful fundraiser.
T	F	I want to be liked by everyone in my office and organization.
T	F	I give my all to my employer, sometimes to the detriment of my own health, rest, and personal life.
T	F	People tend to confide very private things to me.

Exhibit 4.2. *(continued)*

T	F	I should be able to fix every problem that comes along.
T	F	I'm afraid that someday people will find out I'm not really as capable as they think I am.
T	F	Anything that goes wrong is my fault; anything that goes right is due to luck or chance.
T	F	I should be able to do whatever is asked of me.
T	F	If I don't get along with my boss it's my fault.
T	F	If I am not productive, I am worthless.
T	F	I tend to stay too long in jobs where I am unhappy.

The following information is requested for classification purposes only.
Age range   21–30   31–40   41–50   51–60   61–70
Gender   M   F
Job title _____

Number of years on current job _____
Number of years in fundraising _____

The sampling was predominantly female, not a surprising statistic given the tremendous numbers of women entering the field, with a relatively short time reported in fundraising (74 percent of respondents possessed less than ten years of experience in the profession).

Survey results

If we take the contrarian view and assume that there is no greater attraction to the fundraising profession by ACoAs, then the percentage range of ACoAs in the fundraising profession should be between 12.5 percent (the CAOF measurement) and 25 percent (the NIAAA measurement).

Every respondent would be expected to answer "true" to a few statements. For example, most respondents answered "true" to the statement: "I am very sensitive and responsive to the needs of others."

However, when "true" responses are given to statements such as, "I constantly seek approval and affirmation," or, "I'm afraid that someday, people will find out that I really am not as capable as they think I am," then these are indications of the ACoA personality.

A "true" answer rate of 51 percent (more than half) or higher per survey was considered to typify an ACoA fundraiser. This rate was present in 75.6 percent of survey respondents. If a "true" answer rate of 34 percent (more than a third) or higher is applied, then the percentage of surveys fitting this profile jumps to 98!

From these numbers, it would seem that the ACoA is drawn to the profession. If so, for what reasons?

Raising the questions

In 1983, a young fundraiser began to notice that, during individual conversations with her professional colleagues at a major Midwestern private university, a high number self-identified as ACoAs.

This anecdotal, personal realization led to questions that would not begin to be addressed for nearly 20 years:

1. Are ACoAs drawn to and do they find success in the fundraising profession by employing the survival skills developed in an alcoholic family?
2. Does fundraising, as a profession, attract a greater-than-average percentage of ACoAs than is found in the general U.S. population?

This chapter seeks to open a dialogue regarding what appears to be a predominance of one particular psychological condition in the fundraising profession and how it might actually be advantageous in working with volunteers. The author encourages further investigation with a larger, more scientifically controlled sampling and hopes for additional literature to be created for self-help and identification.

What makes ACoAs good fundraisers?

The traits of a good fundraiser have been identified by numerous researchers (see Table 4.1). But why would an ACoA be particularly

Table 4.1. What makes a good fundraiser?

ACoA or Codependent Trait	Panas	Burnett	Worth/Asp
People pleaser	High touch	X	X
Sensitive to the needs of others	X	X	X
Adapts well		"Double agent"	Fits in
Sets high standards	X	X	
Great sense of responsibility	Rigorous discipline	Commitment	
Extremely loyal	X	X	
Caring attitude	X	X	X
Deny self, serve others	Sacrifice		Stay behind the scenes, remain anonymous
High achiever	Perseverance		
Create strong relationships		X	X
Never satisfied with performance	X		
Hard worker	High energy		
Compassionate	X	X	X

Note: Each author identifies traits somewhat differently. When the actual ACoA word or phrase did not appear, the authors' equivalent word or phrase is noted.

Source: Panas, 1988; Burnett, 2002; Worth and Asp, 1995.

adept at building relationships with volunteers? Four ACoA traits are examined.

ACoAs are hypervigilant to the feelings of others. In working with volunteers, a greater sensitivity to their needs and feelings is an asset because it enables the fundraiser to create a more satisfactory experience for the volunteer. This increased perceptiveness lends itself to reading people beyond their spoken words. The ACoA is good at identifying the passion or pain of an individual because of personal experience with both feelings, even if the ACoA isn't in touch with his or her emotional self.

Jessica (some names have been changed to protect anonymity), a fundraiser and ACoA, feels that she owes a debt of gratitude to her undergraduate alma mater because she received a full-tuition scholarship that enabled her to attend college, which she otherwise might not have been able to do. Her passion lies in higher education and raising money for scholarships, and she shares that strong belief with volunteers with whom she has that in common. Jessica has turned her passion into a successful career that includes raising money to endow scholarships, fellowships, training grants, and other student-support projects.

Peggy, a fiftyish, long-time board member who had recently resigned her seat, met for the first time with Ralph, a new fundraiser, as part of his orientation process. Although Peggy had been part of the institution's life for many, many years, something clicked with Ralph. She opened her heart to him about the death of her sister in relationship to this organization. Her sister was a nun who died while in service to the nonprofit.

Peggy happens to be an alcoholic, and Ralph happens to be an ACoA. Anecdotal coincidence? Her painful revelation provides Peggy with the opportunity to relieve some of the ache associated with her sister's death while supporting an organization to which she had never made a significant gift, even as a board member.

ACoAs tend to be people pleasers. ACoA fundraisers are accustomed to accommodating the requests of volunteers and prospects. Often the ACoA is willing to sublimate personal needs in favor of the good of the cause. A good fundraiser also excels at adapting to a variety of situations and personality types, a characteristic shared by the ACoA.

The high-maintenance volunteer can make demands on the fundraiser to the point of being verbally and psychologically abusive, as in the next example.

"This is a real weakness of mine, trying to please everyone, because I won't stand up for myself, confront anyone, or cause any controversy," confided Jaime, thirty-nine, ACoA. "There was enough conflict growing up. Things were very tense, and you never wanted to make waves because what was already happening was so frightening. . . . I carry a lot of that into the workplace. I'm always afraid the same things will happen: people will get angry, raise their voice. These knee-jerk reactions are embedded in me from childhood."

Jaime also exhibits other ACoA characteristics that hamper her career growth and undoubtedly affect her relationships with volunteers. She is afraid to strike out on her own and break away from a dysfunctional marriage with an alcoholic because she does not believe she can be independent, financially or otherwise. Stuck in a small college town where fundraising opportunities are limited, she has been physically, verbally, and emotionally abused by her boss. She fears even positive change and is bound to the way things were in her family of origin.

Ron, fifty-two, ACoA and recovering alcoholic (another common pairing), shared this: "I hold very high standards for myself, and I tend to focus on the half-empty glass often, particularly as it relates to special events. Some minor detail that would be unnoticeable to anyone else will bother me a great deal. The ACoA elevates people pleasing to an art form, not knowing what to expect."

ACoAs feel responsible for the happiness of volunteers and prospects. This trait of codependency (see Exhibit 4.1 for definition and characteristics) could be helpful as a fundraiser bends over backwards to keep a volunteer happy. The ACoA's innate, caring attitude and extreme loyalty supplement this characteristic.

Bonnie, fifty-nine, ACoA and former wife of an alcoholic (also a common pairing), is extremely loyal to her organization, where she has toiled for nearly eighteen years. Fundraising is just one among her myriad job responsibilities. She is good at fundraising because she relates well to others, but she is continually taken advantage of and abused by the executive director because she is unable or unwilling to stand up for herself. Her belief in the organization's mission and cause restrict her from moving on to another, healthier professional situation. She was capable of removing herself from a dysfunctional marriage because her child was involved, but not a dysfunctional workplace, because the workplace involves just herself, and she believes she's not worthy enough to take care of.

Helping other people is a way to get noticed and increase self-esteem. Alexander "Sandy" Macnab, a fundraising consultant, believes that "ours is not a speaking role" for the good fundraiser. The successful fundraiser remains in the background to promote the volunteer or top-level administrators. Success is always attributed to the volunteer or CEO. The authority figures prominent in the "family" workplace dynamic—volunteers, board members, donors, and so on—may or may not recognize the fundraiser's critical role in creating a successful program. At a minimum, ACoA fundraisers might receive an intrinsic reward by doing good and "fixing things," reminiscent of their past experiences.

Strangely enough, Hemfelt, Minirth, and Meier, note that "codependency brings with it a kind of radar. . . . Two hundred people mill about in a grand ballroom. One codependent . . . who walks into the room will single out that one other codependent in the crowd. Every time. Beeline" (1989, p. 117).

An ACoA who was vice president of development at a small university found this unusual radar operating when hiring other fundraisers. She was always able to pick out the codependents in the applicant pool!

This uncanny magnetism also enables ACoAs to pick out alcoholics and other substance abusers. Injecting this many layers of dysfunction into personal and professional relationships with volunteers and colleagues triangulates the interpersonal dynamics to the point that it's amazing anything is accomplished at all!

In its broadest sense, codependence describes individuals who organize their lives—decision making, perceptions, beliefs, values—around someone or something else (Brown, 1988). Adult children of alcoholics grow up codependent. The phrase "adult children" is appropriate because we are old enough in years to be called adults, yet some of us are young enough emotionally to be called children (Woititz and Garner, 1990).

Why would an ACoA choose fundraising as a profession?. Fundraising may be classified as a helping profession, similar to counseling, medicine, and other work, because fundraisers help volunteers and prospects alleviate their pain or celebrate their passion by facilitating involvement with a nonprofit organization.

"Having my needs negated (as a child) made me that much more cognizant of other people's needs, because I don't feel my parents were sensitive or responsive to my needs. As a fundraiser, it makes it easier for me to put myself in other people's shoes," said Bonnie. "It helps me to understand their values, interests, and philosophies, and as a result I can identify common ground between the donor and me."

Helping professions tend to attract people with unresolved codependency issues of their own (Hemfelt, Minirth, and Meier, 1989). A career choice as a helping professional allows us to carry over our sense of responsibility and intense involvement (or overinvolvement) with others (Brown, 1988), including and perhaps especially with volunteers.

Maria served as chair of the fundraising committee, and she worked closely with Alice, the fundraiser. Maria was always punctual, returned phone calls, responded quickly to e-mail, and was overall very dependable.

Suddenly all that changed. Alice offered a variety of solutions to help Maria fulfill her role and make the job easier, but Maria was unresponsive. Finally, Alice met with Maria to see if Maria even wanted to continue in her volunteer role.

Maria self-disclosed that one of her children was experiencing severe mental illness and had been hospitalized. Her husband was an active alcoholic, and she revealed that they had been in and out of couple's counseling their entire marriage. Maria believed that she was suffering from depression.

Alice felt it was safe to share personal information with Maria and revealed that she, too, suffered from depression. She even recommended that Maria ask her doctor about certain medications. For several weeks, Alice felt the need to call Maria to inquire about her and her family's well-being. They shared additional private information. Alice's interest was genuine if not misplaced.

Unfortunately, when a moment arrived that Alice needed Maria's support on an issue and counted on her backing, these intimate conversations did not make Maria any more inclined to support Alice. If anything, Maria felt that Alice knew too much about her.

How many fundraisers allow themselves to be "on call" twenty-four/seven? Nights, weekends, breakfasts, funerals, hospital visits—how often do job responsibilities come before family or personal priorities? The three planned-giving officers at one organization were referred to by their colleagues as Chief Gravediggers 1, 2, and 3 because they were so often seen in dark suits heading to donors' funerals.

Frequently, people who are driven by codependency to rescuing others become adamant in their refusal to take care of themselves:

"Deny self; serve others" (Hemfelt, Minirth, and Meier, 1989). This attitude could be viewed as part of a religious model of service or even martyrdom, but the denial of personal needs can be taken to extreme.

The more severe the crisis, the more present and available we become to "help out." Do you insert yourself as part of the biological family when things take a turn for the worse? Do you sit vigil with family members outside the ICU? Ask yourself, is this a requirement noted on your job description? Or do you interpret this role through "other duties as assigned"? Yet we do these things voluntarily out of a sense of duty and respect, well-intentioned but possibly misplaced.

Every good fundraiser develops close relationships with volunteers. This is not to suggest that these kinds of interactions should be avoided. But when these intense relationships begin to be at the expense of our family and personal life, then they are dysfunctional. Where do we and where should we draw the line between our professional responsibilities and codependent behavior with volunteers?

Bruce was the largest individual contributor to ever make a gift to David's nonprofit. David was the president who worked with Bruce on the gift. Bruce, however, had been an active alcoholic in his younger days, and he had already had one organ transplant because of the physical damage caused by the alcohol.

Now Bruce needed a second transplant. He was in grave condition in the ICU. David appointed himself as the main conduit of information to a wide group of people, including those unrelated to his institution, regarding Bruce. The family was actually relieved to have the burden lifted of returning phone calls and keeping others at bay. David spent countless hours with the family at the hospital and in Bruce's home. He felt that he played a large role in the family's affairs.

However, when Bruce died and people were selected to eulogize Bruce, David was left out, just as he had been left out of milestone events in his own family.

Familiarity, and therefore comfort, with even a negative "family environment" in the field is part of this theory. Who among the profession has described the nonprofit fundraising environment as chaotic, whether in jest or all seriousness?

Chaos is one of the most prominent features of an alcoholic family environment, either overt or covert (Beletsis and Brown, 1981).

Many of us have developed a high tolerance for pain and insanity, abuse, mistreatment, and boundary violation (Beattie, 1989). "Sometimes it has to hurt long and hard before we know it's hurting. . . . Boundaries emerge from deep decisions about what we believe we deserve and don't deserve" (Beattie, 1989).

Jessica, forty-two and the former wife of another ACoA (the "ballroom/radar syndrome"), believes that some of her fundraising experiences adversely affected her mental health. "I allowed myself to be abused by board members. I sought therapy and spent at least three years just trying to address those relationship issues," she admitted. "After more time 'on the couch,' I realized that I don't deserve to be treated poorly in my personal or professional life. I am now able to recognize dysfunctional relationships, and I can make a decision to leave a job before I become ill from it!"

We seek to repeat the past by recreating the family dynamics, but we somehow believe we will get it right this time and fix it (Hemfelt, Minirth, and Meier, 1989). This is usually impossible. An oft-quoted definition of insanity is doing the same thing over and over again but expecting different results. It's one of Ron's favorites!

As a method of coping with the dysfunction in our family of origin, we adopt skills that lend themselves to developing, at the very least, a false intimacy with volunteers and prospects. Some ACoAs yearn for a fantasized sense of closeness (Brown, 1988).

At best, our adaptive mechanisms create valid, strong relationships on behalf of our organization. Niven notes that many ACoAs are high achievers, model children, whom he calls "invulnerables." He states there is "now a tendency to look for positive outcomes, or the benefits of growing up with an alcoholic parent" (1984, p. 3).

Brown, however, believes that these same "positives" become maladaptive and restrictive for the ACoA, with compulsion fueling the high achiever. Brown believes that the search for a positive outcome is in the "service of defense" (1988, p. 30).

In other words, the ACoA takes the adaptive behaviors that allowed him or her to survive childhood and implements these behaviors as an adult in the workplace. However, like many other things, the ACoA doesn't know when enough is enough, or when it's time to stop, and just keeps striving impossibly for greater acceptance, perfection, and reward.

Fundraisers tell a wide variety of stories about how they came to the profession. Ron's is probably more unique than some, however. The son of an alcoholic father, his introduction to fundraising came while he was a practicing alcoholic. Another fundraiser, an active alcoholic, seduced him while they were both drug-impaired, then hired Ron to work for him.

Was this Ron's search gone awry to find and fix his father-figure? Fortunately, after three decades in this profession, Ron has become a consummate fundraiser who is now CEO of a nonprofit.

Cynthia, a fiftyish volunteer and widow, was wildly enthusiastic about a fundraising awards banquet after she first attended it. The organization's fundraiser, an ACoA, harnessed Cynthia's energy by asking her to serve as the chair for the following year's event. However, during subsequent meetings with Cynthia at preview parties, food tastings, and other social activities where alcohol was present, the fundraiser quickly realized that Cynthia was an alcoholic. This realization gave the fundraiser a sinking feeling in the pit of her stomach and created a great deal of anxiety throughout the remainder of the event planning and production. By choosing Cindy as an authority figure she had unconsciously replicated her family of origin.

Unanswered questions

1. Fundraisers have an average job tenure of around eighteen months. Is the reason they tend to change jobs so often because of the ACoA's inability to see a project through to completion? Or is it the Quixotic search for the "something" that is missing or lacking in their life?

2. ACoAs, either through nature or nurture, may be predisposed to becoming substance abusers or may exhibit other addictions,

such as gambling, sex, or work. Does the social nature of the fundraising work environment, complete with alcohol and the perceived reward for working longer than a "normal" work week, encourage or support ACoA addictions?

3. Are other categorical groups of people who possess a "different" sensitivity equally adept at developing relationships and therefore apt to be more prevalent in fundraising (for example, men versus women, gays and lesbians, or current/former religious vocations)?

4. Despite the dysfunctional nature of an ACoA's personal background, the ACoA fundraiser can be quite successful. What sets one ACoA fundraiser apart from another to create triumph from tragedy?

5. As we recruit volunteers, do we subconsciously seek out, attract, and involve the individuals who help us to replicate our dysfunctional family dynamic?

6. How might we work differently with volunteers if we responded in a non-codependent, daresay healthy, way?

Conclusions

Based on preliminary data, one personality type that appears to be predominant in the fundraising profession is the ACoA. (See Addendum for additional personality types that may also be explored through future research.)

The technical skills that enhance a fundraiser's success with volunteers can be learned; personality cannot be taught. The rough edges on an individual's personality can be smoothed, however. Behaviors can be recognized, modified, and even unlearned, to be replaced by appropriate actions. To engage volunteers on behalf of our nonprofit requires a fundraiser with the right personality.

People with technical skills, such as accountants and writers, can be hired to complement and supplement the skills that the fundraiser does not possess. Assume, then, that a fairly even playing field exists in regard to an individual's ability to provide a nonprofit organization with the technical aspects of fundraising, either through the person's personal skills or by hiring the right support team.

Therefore, the varieties in personality type must account for the major differences between a successful and an unsuccessful fundraiser in working with volunteers.

The successful ACoA fundraiser seems to maximize his or her adaptive survival skills to create a rewarding career in a field that requires sensitivity, hard work, flexibility, compassion, and, overwhelmingly, an unfailing ability to develop relationships with many different kinds of volunteers.

The chaotic nature of many nonprofit organizations replicates the family environment in which an ACoA was reared. People are inherently attracted to those things that are familiar and comfortable, even if unhealthy, unless these behaviors are recognized and corrected. Replicating this kind of environment in the workplace gives the ACoA an opportunity with volunteers, whether it's conscious or subconscious, to fix the family dynamic.

Thus, the chaotic nature of the nonprofit world attracts ACoA fundraisers because they believe they at least know what to expect, even if it's bad: constant change and fluctuation; unpredictable behavior from authority figures such as volunteers, gift prospects, and even administrators; and ever-increasing demands for perfection, goal achievement, and performance.

Addendum

There are other measures of the personality types that are attracted to, and may excel at, fundraising and working with volunteers. Two are described herein.

Measurement 1

Some would counter that these traits are also found in Type A personalities, and that one could mistake a Type A personality for an ACoA. However, Type A personalities do not exhibit certain characteristics that ACoAs present, and therefore this argument is invalid.

Type A behavior must have two observable principal behaviors that will distinguish them from an ACoA:

1. Time urgency (or time impatience)
2. Free-floating (all pervasive and ever-present) hostility (Sharma, 1996).

In addition, hostility and anger are the main traits of a Type A personality (Jerabek, 2002). Other characteristics generally not present in the ACoA include the following:

3. Signs of personal tension
4. Personal commitment to having, rather than being
5. Unawareness of the broader environment
6. Strong need to be an expert on a subject, with an otherwise lack of involvement
7. Compulsion to be with other Type A's
8. Speech characterized by explosive acceleration and accentuation of the last few words of a sentence
9. Chronic sense of being in a hurry (Stephens, 1998)

Measurement 2

The Myers-Briggs Type Indicator (MBTI) offers other personality types to which the ACOA can be compared. Isabel Briggs Myers and Katherine Cook Briggs began developing the MBTI in the early 1940s to make Carl Jung's theory of human personality understandable and useful in everyday life (Association for Psychological Type, 2003).

Myers-Briggs relies on four personality dimensions, represented by letters that are combined to create a four-part indicator. The four dimensions are: (1) Extravert (E) or Introvert (I); (2) Sensing (S) or Intuiting (N); (3) Thinking (T) or Feeling (F); and (4) Judging (J) or Perceiving (P).

Described in another way, the MTBI looks at four preferences: (1) Where, primarily, does the individual direct energy? (2) How does the individual process information? (3) How does the individual prefer to make decisions? (4) How does the individual prefer to organize his or her life? (Myers, 1997).

These four-letter type descriptions summarize underlying patterns and behaviors common to most people of that type (Association for Psychological Type, 2003). However, the MBTI is more scientific than suggesting the use of an individual's astrological sign as an indicator of generalized personality. Various tests are conducted to reveal an individual's innate response. These testing instruments are administered by practitioners who must be prequalified in order to purchase the testing materials.

Ideally, the test administrator has training specifically in the psychometric properties and interpretation of the MBTI. There is also a code of ethics regarding the appropriate uses of the MBTI, similar to the code of ethics adopted by the AFP.

Typifying the one or two four-letter personality models that best or most represent the ACoA is difficult, if not impossible.

For example, it can be argued that a good fundraiser is intuitive, idealistic, sensitive, and creative (based on Kiersey, 1998). The MTBI corollaries are quite contradictory. N (Intuition) and S (Sensing) are the polar opposites on the MTBI scale.

But does this mean that a good fundraiser is not also thoughtful, rational, feeling, and a good steward or guardian of the public trust? The MTBI corollaries here are T (Thinking) and F (Feeling), again competing dimensions on the Myers-Briggs model.

References

American Journal of Public Health, Jan. 2000 (entire issue).

Association for Psychological Type. "What Is the Myers-Briggs Type Indicator (MBTI)?" Glenview, Ill.: Association for Psychological Type, 2003.

Beattie, M. *Beyond Codependency: And Getting Better All the Time.* Center City, Minn.: Hazelden Foundation, 1989.

Beattie, M., *Codependent No More: How to Stop Controlling Others and Start Caring for Yourself.* Center City, Minn.: Hazelden Foundation, 1992.

Beletsis, S., and Brown, S. "A Developmental Framework for Understanding the Adult Children of Alcoholics." *Focus on Women: Journal of the Addictions and Health*, 1981, 2, 41–57.

Brown, S. *Treating Adult Children of Alcoholics: A Developmental Perspective.* Wiley: New York, 1988.

Burnett, K. *Relationship Fundraising: A Donor-Based Approach to the Business of Raising Money*. (2nd ed.) San Francisco: Jossey-Bass, 2002.

Friends in Recovery. *The 12 Steps for Adult Children*. Curtis, Wash.: RPI, 1996.

Hemfelt, R., Minirth, F., and Meier, P. *Love Is a Choice: The Groundbreaking Book on Recovery for Codependent Relationships*. Nashville, Tenn.: Thomas Nelson, 1989.

Jerabek, I. "Hostility a Better Predictor of Heart Disease Than Cholesterol Levels, Obesity and Even Smoking: Gauge Your Risk with the New Type A Personality Test from Queendom.com." [http://www.queendom.com/about/media/release22.html], Dec. 2, 2002.

Kiersey, D. *Please Understand Me*. Del Mar, Calif.: Prometheus Nemesis, 1998.

Krisberg, W. *The Adult Children of Alcoholics Syndrome*. New York: Bantam Books, 1988.

Myers, S. "Working Out Your Myers-Briggs Type." [http://www.teamtechnology.co.uk], 1997.

Niven, R. "Children of Alcoholics: An Interview with NIAAA Director." *Alcohol, Health and Research World, 8*(4), 1984.

Panas, J. *Born to Raise*. Chicago: Pluribus Press, 1988.

Sharma, V. P., "Characteristics of a 'Type A' Personality." Cleveland, Tenn.: Mind Publications, 1996.

Stephens, G. K. "Characteristics of a Type A Personality," lecture, Texas Christian University, Dec. 4, 1998.

Woititz, J. G. *The Self-Sabotage Syndrome: Adult Children in the Workplace*. Deerfield Beach, Fla.: Health Communications, 1989.

Woititz, J. G., and Garner, A. *Lifeskills for Adult Children*. Deerfield Beach, Fla.: Health Communications, 1990.

Worth, M. J., and Asp, J. W. "The Development Officer in Higher Education: Toward an Understanding of the Role." *ERIC Digest*. Washington, D.C.: ERIC Clearinghouse on Higher Education, 1995. (ED 382106)

REBECCA E. HUNTER (FORMERLY FINES FOURNIER) *is chief development officer for the American Thoracic Society and a graduate of AFP's Faculty Training Academy. She is author of several articles and designer of seminars, including "Taming the Time Vultures," Writing for Development, Creating New Centers of Influence, and a variety of major gift workshops. She is an ENTJ and has calmed her Type A tendencies.*

*Exploring challenges unique to small nonprofits as
they work with volunteers engaged in fundraising
must start with an understanding of what is meant
by "small" and with other factors besides size. In
some ways, being small has its advantages.*

5

Fundraising volunteers in small organizations

Kenneth J. Knox

CONSIDERABLE HEALTHY DIALOGUE has taken place over the years
regarding the fundraising differences between small and large nonprofits in regard to how they raise funds, and especially how volunteers are involved in the process. Sessions appear on the agendas
of various fundraising conferences identified as "the small shop,"
"emerging organizations," or "grassroots fundraising," implying
that there are, indeed, practices and experiences unique to smaller
organizations.

Does this delineation also imply that the process differs in the
way that smaller organizations recruit, prepare, and supervise
fundraising volunteers? This chapter explores that topic.

The problem with simplification

This subject is often discussed as if only two categories of organizations exist—the small ones and the big ones. But it is not this

NEW DIRECTIONS FOR PHILANTHROPIC FUNDRAISING, NO. 39, SPRING 2003 © WILEY PERIODICALS, INC.

simple. Four distinct categories of charitable causes can be quanti-
fied by the way they are organized and operated and by the pre-
vailing strategies they use to sustain operations:

- Truly *grassroots* organizations
- Structurally organized nonprofits
- Locally institutionalized nonprofits
- Nationally institutionalized nonprofits.

Within each category dwell subcategories, and there are myriad
exceptions when the distinguishing characteristics are explored in
detail, as outlined in Table 5.1.

More than size matters!

Delineation by size (usually signified by budget and number of
employees) is not a totally meaningful way to analyze how volunteers
are engaged in fundraising. Volunteers are significantly impacted by
such variables as the organizational structure, mission, fundraising
strategies, motivation, and a nonprofit's intended audience.

That is, to compare how volunteers are utilized in fundraising
for an organization of less than a $1 million budget and 50 employ-
ees, versus one with a $50 million budget and 1,000 or more
employees, it is important to consider differences other than size.

An upstart grassroots organization is driven by volunteers dedicated to a cause who scramble around to find resources to support
it. They do it because of personal commitment and their author-
ship roles.

Many nationally institutionalized organizations (NIOs) depend
on professional development staff (incidentally, whose jobs are at
stake when fundraising does not meet expectations), not volunteers,
for many technical functions central to their fundraising, although
they might utilize influential volunteers to attract major gifts in
recognition that peer pressure operates at this level. People give to
people like themselves.

Table 5.1. Categories and distinguishing characteristics of charitable causes

Category	Distinguishing Characteristics
Grassroots Organizations	• Typically not registered with IRS, thus not required to file 990; nor subject to CPA audit. • Usually driven by volunteers to fill an emerging need, without paid staff. • May have "rules of operation" or guidelines, and some may be chartered by State, but normally not registered with governmental agencies to perform fundraising. • May be adjunct to a larger organization, such as a faith group, or loosely organized, such as a neighborhood association focused on internal interests, advocacy, or security issues. • May address a project or pressing issue(s) without necessarily planning to expand their mission or become institutionalized beyond current focus; seldom have formal budgets; work mostly off informal, project-based planning, and raise money around projects. • Leadership provided by hands-on volunteers with passion for the cause. • Founders remain involved for long period and eventually yield active role to other volunteers, but retain behind-the-scenes influence. • Fundraising through special events/benefits, individual dues/pledges, and business gifts from people close to the cause. • Unlikely to have a Web page or other formal marketing tools (such as a case statement or brochure).
Structurally Organized Nonprofits	• Grassroots group that has expanded its mission and gained long-range view of itself because of successes or newly emerging issues, or a consciously organized group with the assistance of some outside force or intermediary that has responded to local leadership to address a perceived gap in services. • More formally constituted with bylaws, State charters, and 501(c)(3) status [or (c)(4) or (c)(6)]. • Limited use of fundraising registration laws and IRS gift substantiation requirements. • Modest number of paid staff relative to the task. • Executive director assumes development responsibilities or has part-time or limited development staff. • If created by an outside force or intermediary, receives ongoing technical assistance, sometimes start-up funding, and branding/identification/sanction of the "parent" organization.

Table 5.1. (*continued*)

Category	Distinguishing Characteristics
Structurally Organized Nonprofits (*continued*)	• In some cases, operates like franchise without its own IRS status and seeks local volunteers to serve on "advisory boards" that raise money; although more often are independent of the intermediary and governed by local boards that must raise funds. • Spotty utilization of Internet for fundraising with no Web site or one that is seldom updated, and limited marketing materials. • Utilizes select (targeted) mail rather than direct (mass) mail; heavy emphasis on earned income. • No endowment; limited reserve funds. • Lacks broad visibility.
Locally Institutionalized Nonprofits	• Local or regional focus. • Paid staff, sometimes numbering in the hundreds, characterized by "subsidiaries" to meet needs auxiliary to the core mission (own foundation, spin-off corporations, alumni associations, and for-profit subsidiaries, for example). • Aware of regulations pertaining to fundraising. • Diversified development plan, including formalized planned giving program (possible addition of commercial gift program) managed by development department. • Active grant writing for projects and indirect costs to support operations. • Utilizes telemarketing. • Typically conducts an annual signature special event.

- Limited direct (mass) mail techniques but active mailing/soliciting to alumni, former clients, or other "known" persons
- Occasional capital campaigns.
- Owns endowment and reserve fund of modest size or working toward same.
- Modest or significant name recognition.
- Governance board as well as honorary group of CEO-type fundraising advisers.
- Staff person(s) devoted to volunteer recruitment, training, and supervision.
- Emerging or significant use of Internet.

Nationally Institutionalized Nonprofits

- Paid management and development department(s).
- Endowment handled by Foundation or other management-level personnel.
- Conducts active in-house or out-sourced direct (mass) mail program; uses telemarketers.
- Diversified development plan with several annual giving strategies and periodic capital campaigns; offers formal planned giving expertise.
- Regional/district offices with advisory boards/committees that may or may not have separate IRS status.
- Utilizes localized volunteers and persons with regional name recognition to raise money.
- Prestigious national board.
- Fundraising heavily staff-driven.
- Well-designed Web site and utilization of Internet techniques for seeking volunteers and gifts.
- Modest to high name recognition.
- Services extended to all or many states, and some serve internationally.

Grassroots groups have neither staff to handle technical functions such as research, grant writing, and data collection nor access to prominent volunteers on the same scale. This comparison demonstrates that variables such as the organizational development stage, strategies used, targeted audience, and motivation are determining factors—not size. As we shall also see, groups seeking a national audience are not necessarily large, and being a grassroots group does not equate with being small.

The annual "Philanthropy 400 Survey" published by *The Chronicle of Philanthropy* (2002) lists organizations with the highest income in 2001, many deriving their income from or serving a national audience. Number one is the Salvation Army.

Yet a number of large and small organizations would never make this high-income list although they, too, seek gifts from a broad national audience. Size alone does not define a charity as *national.*

Small does not mean local or disorganized

Certain nonprofit organizations with a national, even international, base have no paid staff, few volunteers, small budgets, and are in an early stage of development. Yet they may be highly organized and professional.

One example is the American Philosophical Practitioners Association (APPA). Four years old with 501(c)(3) status, APPA has a small membership, is governed by a board of five persons, and yet boasts of two advisory boards—one national and one international.

APPA members live in the United States and nine foreign countries. Its office is located within a university department, yet the association's sights are set on broadening its mission to attract an international audience. APPA's Web site outlines a clear mission, written case statement, and ordering information for professional literature.

APPA has volunteer officers but no paid staff and operates on membership dues and a few grants. Although small in terms of budget and staff, APPA is international in scope and is striving to become more institutionalized. Its fundraising volunteers consist of those who created it—its board and advisers.

Clearly, APPA and many nonprofits like it are difficult to pigeon-hole. Because of its sophistication, the group can be described more by its developmental stage than by the usual characteristics of a small organization. Keeping this in mind helps to avoid stereotyping groups that are highly organized on one hand, yet in an early evolutionary stage otherwise.

Impact of organizational development stages

The number and type of volunteers enlisted to help with fundraising is impacted by the nonprofit's stage of development. Each stage requires a different kind of funding strategy and involvement of volunteers.

For instance, when groups are new (whether grassroots or organized), *start up* funding is needed, most often provided in the form of cash or in-kind contributions by the individual(s) who created the organization.

Grassroots groups need funds for spreading the word (to print posters and newsletters, conduct organizational meetings, hire an attorney, and so on). More highly organized groups need money for such things as legal assistance to prepare organizational documents, pay fees to governmental agencies, or perform practical operational activities such as buying office equipment or paying the light bill.

Rarely do volunteers, other than the founder(s), get involved in seeking start-up funding. Although this is expedient at the start, failing to engage many people in the beginning makes it difficult to broaden the fundraising base later. Donors have more enthusiasm when they are in on the ground floor and can shape a new organization. Experiential evidence points to this truth.

As an example, in the formation of the Georgia Affordable Housing Corporation (GAHC), nearly eighty individuals were involved on developmental committees to formulate policies and set direction for a consortium to increase the supply of affordable housing in rural sections of Georgia. When GAHC opened its doors, it had sufficient operating funds for three years plus $55 million in pledged loan funds to finance the construction of apartments in small communities. The bulk of financial support came from those who worked for months on developmental committees to bring GAHC into being.

As groups mature, more sustainable types of resources are required, so they conduct campaigns, create endowments, and move into planned giving. They also undertake special events that require dozens, if not hundreds, of volunteers. In comparison, grassroots groups may be able to round up large numbers of individuals for political support (such as voters to attend a hearing), but generally, few of these persons will be involved in fundraising. Many times there is no staff to recruit and organize additional fundraising volunteers at the grassroots stage of development.

Mature community development organizations, for instance, seek millions of capital dollars to create revolving loan funds to assist low-income households with repairs/rehab loans or first mortgages. Since these groups need "big bucks," regrettably, they may shun all individual fundraising, and turn to foundation and government grant writing. Fundraising for capital, then, becomes staff driven, while board members are underutilized. Once successful in this mode, it is tempting to become overdependent on a small number of corporate donors such as banks and insurers for annual giving, to utilize earned income from housing development activities, and to pay little attention to other annual giving strategies—particularly individual solicitation. This example demonstrates that fundraising volunteerism is impacted by factors other than size. In this case, the compelling factors are the mission and what is perceived, under the circumstances, as efficiency of limited strategies.

Fundraising strategy makes the difference

One major factor regarding the use of volunteers is the kind of activity a nonprofit undertakes. The scope of strategies such as special events, one-on-one solicitation, direct (mass) mail, select (targeted) mail, telemarketing, and corporate campaigns all impact volunteerism.

Some organizations use no volunteers to raise money, and it is not necessarily true that the largest ones utilize a greater number. One would expect that a grassroots group might pull off a rummage sale with three to ten volunteers who bring together their used clothing and household goods to sell. The March of Dimes, on the other hand, seeks thousands of volunteers for its *WalkAmerica*.

At the other extreme, the Boise (Idaho) Neighborhood Housing Services, with a staff of twenty-five and fundraising income of $450,000 (omitting earned income), enlists 3,000 volunteers each spring for its "Paint the Town," an event that provides community service and raises money. Each fall, 3,000 people volunteer for "Rake Up Boise."

Many large organizations with hundreds of employees raise money through staff effort, minimally involving volunteers. Although the size of the organization might make a difference, it is the *nature* of the fundraising activity that constitutes the real difference in how small or large groups utilize volunteers for fundraising.

What is unique to small organizations?

Feedback from an informal survey of small organizations, combined with responses solicited from fundraising consultants who provide services to small organizations, revealed a list of challenges more common to grassroots and emerging or structurally organized groups.

It is worth restating that these characteristics are not true for all small organizations. Incidentally, respondents often equated the word *volunteer* with *board member*, signaling another issue: many nonprofits fail to enlist people beyond their board.

1. *Small organizations seek out few volunteers beyond those who serve on the board and board committees.* With limited staff to recruit, prepare, supervise, and reward fundraising volunteers, volunteers feel

they are "thrown to the wolves" without sufficient preparation or marketing tools to give them comfort to answer donors' questions or make personal solicitations. Participating in manageable special events is less threatening. Larger organizations employ staff to focus on research, maintain records to document service-delivery success that is important to grant seeking, meet with potential donors, and focus on management of volunteers for nontechnical functions.

2. *Volunteers from small organizations do not see themselves as "movers and shakers," opinion leaders, or centers of influence.* Although they may be comfortable selling raffle tickets or asking a local merchant for a door prize, they are ill at ease in calling on a corporate CEO or an individual of a higher financial status. This self-image limits the kinds of fundraising that volunteers are willing to do.

3. *Board and other involved volunteers of small organizations do not contribute personal funds.* A culture of personal giving has not been created, and such requests are met with the response that they give the gift of personal time (which INDEPENDENT SECTOR values for 2002 at $16.54 per volunteer). "You want me to give money, too?" the volunteer asks incredulously. Yet by not contributing financially, they find it hard to ask others to give.

4. *Volunteer boards of small organizations do not understand nor embrace their fundraising responsibilities, have little understanding of where funds come from, and know little of the philanthropic process.* They are unaware that most private giving comes from individuals who are not wealthy (and thus are accessible to them), so they depend on staff to write letters and send grant proposals to companies, government, and foundations.

5. *Unless volunteers are attracted to a small group because of its mission and their closeness to it, they are apt to serve larger organizations with name recognition as their personal position and reputation rise over time.* These upwardly mobile individuals are likely to have developed valuable linkages in the community important in fundraising, yet are not available to serve smaller groups. One consultant related a story about a visit with an officer of a major grocery chain, who confessed that he was in line to become a member of the symphony board and would leave the board of a local theater group as one signal of his rise in the corporate world.

6. *Grassroots and emerging groups lack a broad or readily identifiable base from which to draw volunteers.* They have no alumni or former patients with the ability to give gifts and time that is common to a university or hospital, for instance, or wealthy patrons of the established arts and culture groups. Their boards are typically "working boards" as opposed to the prestige types that are composed of high-level people with influence and connections. Small groups are less likely to have subsidiaries such as an operating foundation (with yet another board), alumni association, and auxiliary groups that attract additional volunteers. To be sure, small groups can attract volunteers to help with demonstrations, programs, or clerical tasks, but these are usually volunteers without substantial financial capacity.

Further challenges

Although other challenges were cited as unique to small organizations, they are actually more universal.

Volunteers lack:

- time to get involved
- knowledge on how to make the "ask"
- clarity regarding the fundraising role before joining the board
- understanding that giving satisfies donors' needs
- a strategic or development plan to see where they fit into the scheme of things and how important volunteers are to the plan's success

Volunteers also:

- abdicate their fundraising role to the staff
- are asked to perform work too demeaning for their station in life when it involves small tasks
- fear failure
- become unexcited about fundraising strategies due to lack of involvement in the planning
- may be involved in so many causes that they feel it is impossible to raise or give money for each one

Some of these universal challenges may be difficult for small organizations to carry out as well as their larger counterparts, simply because of the absence of sufficient paid personnel.

For example, a well-planned and conducted fundraising orientation will help volunteers overcome their reluctance to make a personal request for a donation, and will provide them with the knowledge that there is a "values exchange" between donors and institutions—that is, donors receive a psychic, political, or material benefit when they give. Such training is important for all sizes of organizations, but to the extent that larger nonprofits have staff assigned to this function, they have an advantage over smaller groups without the same staff capacity.

Advantages enjoyed by small organizations

Charitable causes that remain local and are directed toward ameliorating an issue important to a community have an advantage in recruiting volunteers to help with fundraising. Just as companies advertise "locally owned and operated" as a marketing tool, small or localized organizations can use a similar underlying idea to recruit nonpaid workers.

The closer volunteers feel toward a cause—the more passionate they are—the more likely they will be motivated to support it. Studies done by INDEPENDENT SECTOR (IS) reveal a high correlation between individuals who volunteer time for an organization and those who give to it.[1] Information from IS's *The New Nonprofit Almanac, IN BRIEF, 2001*, graphically illustrates that households that both gave money and volunteered gave an average of $1,339 in 1998, two-and-one-half times the $524 average contribution from households that did not volunteer (INDEPENDENT SECTOR, 2001).

Another advantage enjoyed by local groups is that it is easier for volunteers to walk into the office of a local organization and provide services than it is for a regional or national group to expect volunteer workers to travel over great distances to do the same.

In spite of these advantages, the challenge is for small or localized organizations to devote time and marketing tools to recruit individuals, provide them with orientation/training and supervision, and reward them for their service. A common dilemma is how to prioritize this management function while continuing to deliver services and programs.

Tips for small and newly developed shops

This chapter's assertion is that size must be considered along with the stage of development and other variables to more accurately explore the role of volunteers in fundraising. The tips provided here speak primarily to organizations characterized as grassroots or structurally organized. These tips also can be profitable for more institutionalized organizations interested in exploring basic principles or reviewing possible reasons why they lack success in attracting more volunteers.

Tip 1. Focus on resource development rather than fundraising

Resource development includes a recognition that involving people and creating a favorable image are integral to raising money. To gain this broader perspective, it is critical that the Chief Professional Officer (executive director) or the Chief Voluntary Officer (board chair) receive some training in the philanthropic process. These leaders must first view volunteers as *human capital* and then help volunteers learn to articulate the value of the mission. Achieving this training takes time away from other management and organizational duties but must be placed on par with delivering services to the public.

One practical solution to the time-constraint issue is to find a head volunteer that will coordinate other volunteers so that leadership's time is more efficiently spent relating to this one person. A solution for grassroots groups that need leaders trained in fundraising is to find local resources for this. Examples are learning from other nonprofits, regional associations of grant makers (RAGS), nonprofit centers, United Way, local chapters of the Association of Fundraising Professionals, and applying for scholarships from various sources.

Tip 2. *Understand that "volunteers really don't volunteer"*

Although perhaps an overstatement, the underlying concept is that a specific leader must be in charge of organizing, directing, motivating, and assisting nonpaid persons to do the job they said they would do. Many times we hear staff say, "The board (volunteers) just won't do what they committed to!"

This assertion does not allow for good intentions to be interrupted by the realties of work, home life, and social demands on volunteers who may find a role more overwhelming than they originally thought. It is incumbent on the leader to remind them of the tasks, offer to help, and even provide ghostwriting or other support. This is not creating dependency but providing volunteers with a taste of success so they will do more.

Leaders are kidding themselves if they expect the typical volunteer to *initiate* activity without direction, especially if the activity requires original research and writing. One consultant noted less than a dozen exceptions to this over a lifetime of working with nonprofits, in which an extraordinary volunteer actually pushed or challenged the staff or leader to keep up.

A practical solution to improving volunteer performance is to spend time outlining job responsibilities connected to fundraising strategies and enlisting board members willing to provide orientation to new volunteers. For instance, if telemarketing will be utilized to upgrade gifts from current donors, leaders must provide volunteers with tools for success:

- Prepare a list of donors with past giving history.
- Draft a suggested script.
- Secure facilities to make the calls.
- Provide suggestions to deal with potential responses.
- Create a fact sheet on the organization.
- Describe how the organization will use the money.

It is unrealistic to expect volunteers to think of and initiate all these steps without assistance.

Tip 3. Do what is practical, given size of staff and volunteer base

Assuming too many fundraising activities can kill the need to celebrate success. Moreover, chasing dollars because they are available may lead to "mission drift" if the source of funding requires delivery of services unrelated to the core mission.

Focus on the need to build a broad base of annual givers before taking on a capital campaign. Develop a signature special event, and improve it over time rather than conduct a series of many small events that drain volunteers and require heavy staff time. (This may take some experimenting to find the key event that matches the interest of the volunteers, is compatible with the mission, and will be supported by the community.)

Of course, if board members wish to conduct an event of special interest to them, such as aiding a family in need or renovating a neighborhood park, this should be supported, but not in lieu of a harder-hitting money-raising event for unrestricted funds.

Tip 4. Focus effort on "natural constituencies"

Focus on potential donors who have something to gain by supporting your cause, or who have a natural connection, so that volunteers easily see the win-win relationship.

For instance, if an organization is promoting affordable housing, natural constituents are those who benefit from the activity—lenders, insurers, building material providers, construction trades, appraisers, surveyors, architects, closing attorneys/title companies, landscapers, and so on. It would not be as profitable or cost-effective for small organizations to conduct costly mass mailings (including follow-up mailings) to unknown parties as it would be to focus on these natural potential donors.

Tip 5. Create a board-appointed group to help with resource development

Such an option should be considered once a small organization has been in business long enough to build stability. This additional group might be known as an honorary board of trustees, a leadership council, or board of advisers. They have no policy-making authority, meet once or twice a year, and provide periodic entrée and advice.

This is appropriate for individuals with broad civic connections and in key community leadership positions who would be attracted to such a group but do not have time to attend monthly board meetings or personally solicit gifts. They can, however, ensure a company or personal gift, receive updates regarding the organization, and act as goodwill ambassadors.

The Neighborhood Housing Services of Baltimore, Miami, Chicago, New York, and several similar neighborhood-based organizations have created such groups to augment the work of board volunteers.

Overcoming obstacles

Lyrics from an old song say to "accentuate the positive; eliminate the negative" (Mercer, 1944). As grassroots and structurally organized groups look for ways to excite and involve a larger number of volunteers for their fundraising activities, they must learn to accentuate their advantages.

Being local in nature and independent in governance, their mission is likely to be understood and supported if visibility is increased and their needs documented. By spending time getting their message out to the public and marketing to potential clients and sympathizers, the groundwork is established to recruit nonpaid helpers. Volunteers can't give time to something they are unaware of, even if the cause would appeal to their personal set of values.

Location, location, location! Emerging organizations also need to publicize a location and encourage walk-in traffic to maximize convenience. Grassroots groups without an office location may need to spend time seeking a place that can be identified as their own, including displaying a public sign. Volunteers need a base from which to work.

Finally, small and emerging groups must establish a culture of giving from the very beginning, involving their closest supporters. As important as volunteer time is, time alone is not enough. Somebody, somehow, must pay the bills. If such a principle is understood and accepted, volunteers will also be donors and more apt to ask others for financial support.

Accentuating these advantages will not substitute for other steps that must be taken to successfully find and utilize the time of volunteers, but if ignored, will make the job even more difficult.

Summary

Small and emerging nonprofits, operating at various levels of success and numbering in the hundreds of thousands, improve our communities and institutions. They are critical to civic life.

These organizations have small budgets and few employees. Typically, organizations very early in their development and those striving for a higher degree of organization face challenges not easily overcome. Perhaps challenge Number One is finding the time and resources to recruit and manage volunteers for fundraising and other management functions. This is difficult if all emphasis is placed on service or program delivery.

On the positive side, they enjoy certain advantages of being closely connected with their supporters, are usually more accessible, and find a degree of loyalty not enjoyed by larger groups.

As small groups invest in training so that their leaders are grounded in the philanthropic process, their fundraising options will increase. Still, they must stick to fundraising strategies that they are equipped to handle, be realistic in their expectations of what volunteers can or will do, play on their organizational strengths to attract volunteers, and find creative ways to manage them.

In some ways, all nonprofits face similar challenges in working with volunteers. Nevertheless, smaller and emerging groups must overcome obstacles such as lack of visibility, access to high-level volunteers, and engaging staff (or leadership) to center on the proper utilization of human capital.

Note

1. INDEPENDENT SECTOR, an organization formed to celebrate the nonprofit and philanthropic community's unique role in American life, publishes studies, such as "Giving and Volunteering in the United States" (2001, 2000, and previous years). Visit independentsector.org for more information.

References

INDEPENDENT SECTOR. *New Nonprofit Almanac in Brief: Facts and Figures on the Independent Sector 2001*. Washington, D.C.: INDEPENDENT SECTOR, 2001, p. 11.

Mercer, J., and Arlen, H. "Ac-cent-tchu-ate the Positive" (song). New York: Harwin Music Company (managed by MPL Communications), 1944.

"The Philanthropy 400 Survey." *The Chronicle of Philanthropy*, Oct. 31, 2002, 1.

Resources

Books

Klein, Kim. *Fundraising for Social Change*. Berkeley, Calif.: Chardon Press, 1994.

Flanagan, Joan. *The Grass Roots Fundraising Book*. Lincolnwood, Ill.: NTC/ Contemporary Publishing Group, 1995.

Web sites

American Philosophical Practitioners Association (www.appa.edu)

Boise Neighborhood Housing Services (www.boisenhs.org)

Georgia Affordable Housing Corporation (www.georgiaaffordablehousing. org)

INDEPENDENT SECTOR (www.independentsector.org)

Sibbet, David, and Le Saget, Meryem (www.arthuryoung.com/sibbet2.html; takes the reader through stages from "startup" to "co-creation")

KENNETH J. KNOX *is an independent consultant based in Atlanta who specializes in the creation of new organizations and fundraising development for small and emerging nonprofits throughout the country. Clients are often network members supported by national or regional intermediaries. Knox also designs and teaches fundraising workshops and retreats and is an alumnus of the Faculty Training Academy of the Association of Fundraising Professionals.*

Appendix: Medical Society Fund Raising Network

The Medical Society Fund Raising Network (MSFRN) was organized in the mid-1990s when fundraising was still two words, although "organized" is a loosely defined term.

A decade ago, association fundraising was beginning to grow. No single fundraising organization—not the National Society of Fund Raising Executives (now Association of Fundraising Professionals), the Association of Healthcare Professionals (now Association for Healthcare Philanthropy), or the American Society of Association Executives (ASAE)—filled the void felt by several association development officers and a fundraising consultant.

In the time-honored American tradition, they decided that if they wanted the situation addressed, they'd better do it themselves. MSFRN was born.

Invitations to attend the semiannual meetings were by word of mouth. There are still no dues, officers, bylaws, governing board, office, staff, or anything other than a mailing list of attendees that was maintained by one of the founders. The national mailing list is now a bit more high-tech, with an e-mail list-serve replacing snail mail.

The only requisite for membership is that the attendee be involved in fundraising for a medical society, as the MSFRN name implies. Corporate, individual, planned giving, and foundation fundraisers, along with other association executives with fundraising duties, are welcome. Pharmaceutical company representatives who work with some of these fundraisers also attend to offer a corporate perspective. Consultants who attend are barred by mutual agreement from blatant shilling for clients.

New members are identified by current attendees and are added to the list-serve by the current meeting planner. Sometimes current members are allowed to continue attending, even if their fundraising position is no longer with a medical society that works directly with people.

In 2003, thirty-five people attended the winter meeting in Florida. Meetings are organized by a volunteer from the group, and sometimes a different volunteer works with other members to create the program agenda, finding speakers and presenters on a variety of topics pertaining to medical society fundraising. Topics for discussion and potential meeting sites are identified at the end of one meeting in preparation for the following meeting, so that future organizers have some idea of the needs and desires of the group.

A useful function for MSFRN is the occasional benchmarking study or broad spectrum survey conducted by members. Collaborative relationships have grown, based on the interaction of colleagues at the MSFRN. Additional activities include sharing information and publications, problem solving, education, and networking. MSFRN members bring job postings to the meetings, hoping to recruit qualified colleagues.

Industry representatives discuss changes in the corporate and regulatory environments, trends in the industry, and the implications of both on MSFRN members.

All expenses are shared among the attendees, who pay equally for room and board. On occasion, corporate underwriting lowers these costs.

MSFRN is an example of a grassroots yet national organization.

*The preceding chapters examined fundraising vol-
unteers' roles from a large-scale perspective. This
chapter refines the view to a smaller, more localized
level by addressing one subset of organizations—the
small liberal arts college. College and university
fundraising is an area familiar to nearly all professionals in our field, and the use of educational
fundraising as an example helps apply previously
outlined concepts.*

6

The old college try: Volunteers in fundraising efforts for small liberal arts colleges

Jody Abzug, Rikki Abzug

WHAT HAS BEEN, IS, AND SHOULD BE the role of voluntary efforts in college fundraising? While the increasing professionalization of fundraising has institutionalized the role of the certified development office/officer at most of the nation's small liberal arts colleges (and most other institutions of higher education, beyond the purview of this study), there seems little doubt that volunteers are still sought and serve in many of the colleges' outreach efforts. What remains less clear is how colleges best utilize pools of volunteers—mostly alumni.

In this study, we specifically look at the role of voluntary class agents and student solicitors in the effort to improve alumni giving.

NEW DIRECTIONS FOR PHILANTHROPIC FUNDRAISING, NO. 39, SPRING 2003 © WILEY PERIODICALS, INC.

We also discuss the role of student volunteers soliciting senior gifts and the role of the voluntary board.

After first briefly reviewing the history of both higher education fundraising in general and alumni giving efforts in small liberal arts colleges, we will focus on the latest incarnations of efforts to tap alumni dollars. Using a database derived from *U.S. News and World Report*'s latest annual ranking of small liberal arts colleges and telephone interviews with development and alumni-relations officers, this study will look at how "voluntary efforts" correlate with alumni giving.

A short history of volunteer fundraising in higher education

Before the "invention of the nonprofit sector" (Hall, 1992) and the professionalization of fundraising, there were volunteers! One could argue that we have come so far in professionalizing fundraising efforts (the rise of the development office and officer are prime examples) that the role of volunteers has been largely eclipsed and sometimes even forgotten. It is our intention in this chapter to report that volunteer fundraising on (and on behalf of) college campuses (of the top small liberal arts variety) is alive and well, even if not always central to development strategies. Indeed, the voluntary efforts of students, alumni, and boards of trustees have never disappeared, even if they are increasingly managed (sometimes scripted) by and through professional development offices.

The professionalization of college fundraising has occurred over a 350-year history in the United States. Never forgetting the volunteer efforts on behalf of beloved schools, research raises questions about the roles that volunteers play in fundraising today and into the future. To answer these questions, we describe the survey study conducted during the winter of 2002–03. Our results are presented along with a host of successful practices described in detail, and conclude with implications and areas for further inquiry.

Background

Brittingham and Pezzullo (1990) describe four historical trends that have changed higher education fundraising in the United States: (1) the substitution of professional appeals for church-related and individual solicitations, (2) the replacement of charity by philanthropy, (3) the new centrality of fundraising to the activities of college presidents and boards, and (4) the advent of fundraising in public institutions.

This transition to professional strategies has spawned an increasing body of knowledge. The creation of a body of accepted knowledge regarding an occupation is one of the hallmarks of the professionalization of that job.

Much of this literature is aimed at finding correlates of increased fundraising activity. However, research has not had much luck singling out determinant features of fundraising success (Brittingham and Pezzullo, 1990).

Loessin, Duronio, and Borton (1988), for instance, found near unanimity in the types of strategies that 575 universities used. Dunn, Terkla, and Secakusuma (1989) were able to point to size of endowment and operating budget as major factors in raising funds, but they could not explain leverage with their variables. Rooney (1999) has weighed in with the suggestion that measures of fundraising effectiveness themselves need to be revised to take into account previously hidden costs of the professionalization of this function in universities.

One could argue that a fifth trend should be added to those elaborated by Brittingham and Pezzullo (1990)—that of the increasing importance of women as donors and philanthropists in the higher education field (see Tanner and Ramsey, 1993; Ferguson-Patton, 1993). One particularly relevant revelation in the emerging field of women in higher education philanthropy is the idea that, as Ferguson-Patton (1993, p. 69) puts it: "Men will give to become involved . . . whereas women seek to be involved . . . then give." This idea that college stakeholders may seek involvement as a prerequisite to giving leads us to question the roles of various pools of volunteers in the fundraising efforts of educational institutions.

Specifically, what this study attempts is to "bring the volunteers back in" to the picture. While we recognize that the use of volunteers is by no means costless, per Rooney's (1999) concern, we suggest that creative use of volunteers may have fundraising (as well as other) benefits above its costs. To that end, we posed the following research questions pertaining to three main pools of volunteers from which most institutions of higher education (and specifically small liberal arts colleges) can draw. In the fundraising efforts of top liberal arts colleges:

- What are (effective) roles of alumni volunteers?
- What are (effective) roles of student volunteers?
- What are (effective) roles of volunteer boards of trustees?
- What are promising practices for using alumni, student, and board volunteers?

Methodology

To explore our research questions, we created a survey instrument on volunteers' roles in fundraising that we administered to the directors of development offices and alumni relations (depending on where the management of volunteers was headquartered) at small liberal arts colleges[1]. Our population of concern was the *U.S. News and World Report*'s 2002 top 25 small liberal arts colleges in the United States.

We administered the telephone survey during the winter of 2002–03, and we were able to secure completed surveys from 23 of 25 schools for a response rate of 92 percent. We received responses from development or alumni offices at (in alphabetical order): Amherst, Bates, Bryn Mawr, Carleton, Claremont McKenna, Colby, Davidson, Grinnell, Hamilton, Harvey Mudd, Haverford, Middlebury, Mt. Holyoke, Oberlin, Pomona, Smith, Swarthmore,

Trinity, Vassar, Washington and Lee, Wellesley, Wesleyan, and Williams Colleges.

We combined the survey data with *U.S. News and World Report* data on the percentage of alumni who give, that when added to measures of volunteer effectiveness, became our main variable of interest.

Findings

From the descriptive statistics in Table 6.1, we begin to craft a profile of the role of volunteers in small liberal arts college fundraising.

Table 6.1. Telephone survey of 23 U.S. colleges

Variable	N	Minimum	Maximum	Meam	Standard Deviation
Alumni giving rate (% giving)	23	42	65	50.652	6.2349
Are alum volunteers used?	23	1	1	1	0.0000
Are class agents used?	23	1	1	1	0.0000
Are reunion volunteers used?	23	0	1	0.522	0.5108
Number of class agents	23	20	1,400	488.565	429.6707
Number of reunion volunteers	23	0	250	42.381	69.2571
% of alums who volunteer	23	0	9	2.933	2.6067
Effectiveness of alums: 1 (low)–5 (high)	23	2	5	4.239	0.7959
Are student volunteers used?	23	0	1	0.870	0.3444
Are volunteers used for senior gifts?	23	0	1	0.783	0.4217
Number of student volunteers	23	0	620	55.333	133.5613
% of senior body who volunteer	23	0	14	4.554	4.6238
% of student body who volunteer	23	0	26	2.729	5.5727
Effectiveness of students (1–5)	23	2	5	4.263	0.9032
Is the board a "fundraising board"?	23	1	4	3.022	0.8185
Does the board have a give-get policy?	23	1	5	3.864	1.3988
Do most donations come through the board?	23	2	5	2.955	0.8579

We can begin to describe the role of three pools of volunteers: alumni, students, and boards of trustees.

The top small liberal arts colleges standardly make use of alumni volunteers in fundraising. All colleges use alumni as class agents (whether they are called that or not) when soliciting annual gifts. Just over half of the schools have an additional annual program that uses alumni volunteers to help with reunions. The absolute number of class agents used varies widely from a low of 20 to a high of 1,400, with an average of just under 500 agents per school. The schools' solicitable alumni bases (living alumni with valid addresses from whom to draw gifts) ranged from a low of 3,900 to a high of 34,000.

The actual percentage of alumni serving as volunteers (a better test of the extent of alumni involvement in fundraising activity) ranged from a low of .004 percent to a high of 9 percent. Development and alumni-relations officers rank the effectiveness of alumni volunteers from a low of 2 to a high of 5, with an average of 4.24.

Almost 90 percent of the colleges use student volunteers in some manner. Slightly fewer, almost 80 percent, use student volunteers to help solicit senior class gifts. Most of the colleges have determined that, while using students for phone-a-thons/telefunds can continue to be a useful exercise (see Schaeffer, 1990), most have moved away from volunteers and toward paid student labor for this important fundraising tool. The number of students involved in all-volunteer fundraising activities ranges from 0 to 620 (an anomaly based on the use of volunteer student callers), with an average of 55.

The percentage of the senior class involved in soliciting senior class gifts ranged from 0 to 14 with an average of 4.5, while the percentage of the total student body involved in volunteer fundraising ranged from a low of 0 to a high of 26 percent, with an average of 2.7 percent. The effectiveness of student volunteers was ranked just slightly higher than the effectiveness of alumni volunteers, with an average of 4.26 percent, compared to 4.24 percent for alumni. The rankings of effectiveness of both alumni and student volunteers are somewhat higher than development officers' evaluations of their college's boards solely as effective fundraising bodies.

Perhaps given that volunteer fundraising is not seen as the major role of these groups compared with the board, development professionals are more likely to appreciate the work done by alumni and students in an "extra" capacity. The average ranking of boards as "fundraisers" was a 3 out of 5, although the actuality of a board with a give/get policy was closer to 4 (at 3.86). Private money coming to the college through the board averaged a rank of just below 3 on the five-point scale. These rankings suggest room for improvement in enhancing fundraising efforts through volunteers by leveraging their boards.

In addition to the subjective effectiveness rankings of the development and alumni-relations professionals, we sought correlations between the percentage of alumni who give (according to *U.S. News and World Report*) and the various alumni volunteer measures. Running bivariate correlations revealed two significant relationships. The correlation between the percentage of alumni who give and the absolute number of class agents was positive (+.527) and significant at the 0.01 level. This suggests that the greater the (absolute) number of class agents that a college has, the higher the alumni giving percentage.

Likewise, the correlation between the percentage of alumni who give and the percentage of alumni involved in voluntary fundraising was also positive (+.464) and significant, although at the 0.05 level. This suggests that it is also the case that the higher the percentage of alumni who volunteer in fundraising, the higher the alumni giving percentage.

We can't know for sure that the higher percentage of volunteers and the greater number of agents actually produced higher alumni giving, or the other way around, whichever way the causality flows. This still suggests an important role for alumni volunteers in small liberal arts college fundraising. Indeed, it may not be enough just to have alumni involved, if greater levels of involvement are actually correlated with greater percentages of giving alumni. Adhering to the best practice can be bested by bettering the practice!

Along with the statistical analysis, the more qualitative interview portion of our study yielded a number of promising practices, as described in the next section.

Practices proven effective

Academically successful students graduate and become alumni. Successful alumni are prime prospects for helping to give and get financial resources. The acculturation process to develop in young people an understanding of the need to give back must start at the beginning of their college career.

Effective roles for alumni volunteers

While all of the schools surveyed use alumni volunteers for some form of class agent program in their annual fund, the recruitment methods vary. Some staff members recruit all of their class volunteers, while at other schools one alumnus is chosen to head their class's efforts, and he or she is responsible for recruiting others to help. At two of the schools, associate class agents are chosen (voted or selected) for the following year while still enrolled as seniors.

At one college, each person on the development staff manages his or her own cadre of volunteers who fulfill advisory, cultivation, and even solicitation roles. Each officer has five or so alums that they feel comfortable calling to learn more information about prospects in that alum's region. Another college uses alums in prospect-screening sessions.

Still another college utilizes alums as memorial chairs. Memorial chairs identify, cultivate, and in some instances might solicit classmates for gifts in memory of another classmate or in memory of one of their own family members. Some colleges involve volunteers in their solicitations of top prospects. Most often these volunteers are board members, but occasionally they are alums who themselves make high-end gifts.

Several of the colleges use alums as planned giving chairs. These alums help identify classmates (or other alums) who are prospects for planned giving. They will work with the planned giving officer on cultivation. In attempts to get alums to make large contributions, some of the schools employ gift categories or clubs and have alumni volunteers chair a committee to identify, cultivate, and solicit prospects. These committees can be local, regional, or national. Indeed, most of the colleges have alumni clubs in different regions in the country.

At one school, these clubs conduct their own alumni fundraising. Although volunteers at one school did not receive the highest rating for effectiveness, the development officer reasoned that the volunteers' job description needs to be re-vamped. Many alums who are recruited as class agents serve for five years (from reunion to reunion). In 2003, it is difficult to find people who are willing to make a five-year commitment; even if they make the commitment, they may not be effective for the whole time. An alternative is to shorten their term of service.

For most alumni volunteers, there is an acceptable learning curve. Few volunteers are completely effective immediately. Many excel in time, but need a great deal of help, input, and hand-holding by development staff. It is a trade-off. Schools want alumni volunteers to help decrease office work loads, but for the first several years, new volunteers are heavily dependent upon staff support. Many of the schools believe that they should pare down their number of alumni volunteers, clearing the "dead wood," thereby hopefully fostering more overall effectiveness from volunteers.

It is interesting, in light of our empirical findings, that one respondent added that it is far more difficult to be creative when the number of volunteers per class, and the total number of volunteers, increases. According to this development officer, fewer volunteers could be more effective, but again, when there is such a committed group of alumni, staff must be willing to accept all those who wish to volunteer.

Another possibility is to accept all who wish to volunteer but use some volunteers in a limited role. If an alum wishes to be involved but is not an effective solicitor, he/she could be involved in writing letters, personal notes or thank-yous. One college development officer thought their class agent program needed so much revision that it might work better to raise money without volunteers. However, as most staff suggested, alums at these small liberal arts colleges want to and need to be engaged and involved. The class agent programs need to be adjusted so they can be successful.

Indeed, on occasion, the problem lies with staff, not volunteers. These liberal arts colleges have very devoted alumni bases and thus have volunteer-rich environments, but sometimes the staff cannot find relevant jobs or tasks for them, or volunteers are recruited long before they are actually needed, and so their interest wanes.

For some colleges, the biggest obstacle is that their alumni base historically has not been involved with fundraising. For these schools, the immediate challenge is to convert their alums to donors and then to recruit some of them to volunteer and assist with the fundraising.

Promising roles for student volunteers

Many of the schools run senior class gift programs or challenges and even rate student volunteers higher in the category of effectiveness than alums. However, some schools think that the senior year may be too late to get students interested in or involved with philanthropy. The students need an earlier introduction, perhaps in their junior year, to the senior class gift program.

While there is a precedent of paid staff soliciting alumni contributions, it is unrealistic to think that paid staff could effectively solicit students. As one development officer put it, "One can't raise money administratively from students." A successful motivation for increasing senior class gifts is to raise the money for a specific cause, such as scholarships. Another effective way to motivate students is to compare them with their comrades at other similar (perceived competitor) schools. One of the colleges adds this incentive to their senior class gift program, and their students try to raise more money and have a higher participation rate than their comparable schools. For one school that adds its senior class gift program into totals for the annual fund, the senior gifts account for 6 percent of the school's total participation rate.

A few of the schools who do not have a senior class gift program try instead to get seniors thinking about their eventual role as alumni donors by voting or recruiting class agents for their first year out. One college has a unique program to educate students about philanthropy. A program open to all students educates them about the finances of the college. A discussion of the college's finances leads directly into a discussion about alumni giving.

Another college uses an interesting mixture of paid student callers and student volunteers. The latter manage the paid callers. They attend alumni meetings and may even author solicitations. These managers also run their school's senior class gift program.

A third school works with student callers who volunteer for a limited time. On a particular night, the callers are all from the same student organization/group/team. Although not individually paid, the college does give each group financial incentives for being successful. The student group will receive money from the college based on its performance (total dollars raised).

While it seems most colleges have moved away from using student volunteers for calling and have instead turned to paid student callers, student volunteers are utilized by development officers in other nondirect fundraising ways, such as stewardship. One development office involves students in a thank-a-thon, where students are asked to write a number of thank you letters to alumni annual fund donors. Another school has the students add personal notes to its annual fund-solicitation letters.

An area in which students are effective is in capital campaign launches. Students representing different school groups (athletics, scholars, artists, and student leaders) are brought to campaign kickoffs to mingle with alums. These students reflect the college's current student body and are present to speak a little about the college today and to answer group and individual questions. It often is easier for an alum to identify with students than with the college's administration. Students are less likely to give bureaucratic answers and bestow a human element to the campaign. Suddenly, gifts represent students with names and faces. These meetings personalize the campaign and can encourage larger donations.

Finally, students at some schools are involved in other activities, such as trivia challenges, magazine distributions, concessions at sporting events, or the sale of school-tagged items to raise money for student groups. These activities are generally coordinated separately and not directly managed by or affiliated with the formal development office or alumni unit.

Board roles

This study was not designed to explore, in depth, the role of the volunteer board of trustees in fundraising. However, one of the most important legal responsibilities of boards is to ensure the financial position of the organization. We did record observations from development officers and alumni-relations directors.

For instance, some schools involve their board of trustees in phon-a-thons for high-end donors. Other schools who do not have structured phon-a-thons still involve their board members in calling top prospects. And it should be noted that most of the small liberal arts colleges report 100 percent board participation—suggesting very little room for improvement in that department!

Conclusion

Despite the increasing professionalization of fundraising, alumni and student volunteers remain quite effective. For the small liberal arts college, where the concept of class year encourages a sense of cohesion and identity, students should be introduced to the concept of giving back to their alma mater from the moment they are recruited. As these students become alumni, small liberal arts colleges must be diligent in maintaining those linkages that will prove increasingly lucrative in the future. Staff and volunteers are partners in process and progress.

Note

1. At many of the small liberal arts colleges, the alumni volunteers are managed by an alumni council (sometimes called an alumni executive committee). This council includes alums volunteering for their alma mater as fundraisers as well as those who volunteer in other capacities. On occasion, the chair (or head) of the alumni council also sits on the board of trustees, but not always as a voting member. The alumni council is the governing board for the Alumni Association at many of our surveyed colleges.

Infrequently, even alumni council chairs who do not sit on the board of trustees can be voted onto the board because of their voluntary service to the college.

Some of the annual funds are managed by their own board of directors. Most often it is a solo annual giving chair. Annual fund volunteers frequently are supervised by annual fund chairs. In some colleges, alumni volunteers are grouped with current parent volunteers, thus the annual fund chair(s) could be either an alum (a former head class agent) or a parent.

Different schools supply different names for annual fund volunteers. Some of the more common titles are *class agent*, *class representative*, and *class leader*. Typically their role is the same.

Some of the annual fund chairs and their committees are granted the power to determine yearly policies as well as to set overall dollar and participation goals for the entire solicitable alumni base. Often individual class goals are set by those classes' lead agents/volunteers. Other chairs and their committees are strictly advisory. They supply input but neither set the agenda nor determine the year's giving goals. Their titles, such as *fund advisory committee*, emphasize their role.

Some of the colleges have very structured and highly tiered governing groups. Class associate agents report to class head agents, who report to annual fund vice chairs, who report to the annual fund chair. Classes may have five to thirty associate agents, with one to three head agents. Vice chairs are responsible for a couple or several classes. At these schools, a volunteer often moves up the ranks from associate agent to head agent to vice chair. Thus their advice comes from having been intimately involved at each level.

Within the board of trustees (or board of directors), there is often a development (advancement) committee responsible for all fundraising activities. These might include annual fund, major, leadership, and planned giving; and capital and endowment campaigns. Their decisions may be made in conjunction with an alumni council subcommittee or the chairs of the annual fund. When annual fund chairs sit on the board, they are responsible for annual giving reports at each of the board meetings.

References

Brittingham, B. E., and Pezzullo, T. R. *The Campus Green: Fund Raising in Higher Education.* Washington, D.C.: Council for Advancement and Support of Education, George Washington University, 1990.

Dunn, J. A., Jr., Terkla, D. G., and Secakusuma, P. "Fund Raising's Top 100: A Study Identifies and Compares the Most Successful Institutions." *Currents*, 1989, *15*, 50–55.

Ferguson-Patton, K. "Women Talking to Women About Giving: Creating Incentives, Avoiding Resistance." New Directions for Philanthropic Fundraising, no. 2. San Francisco: Jossey-Bass, 1993.

Hall, P. D. *Inventing the Nonprofit Sector and Other Essays on Philanthropy, Voluntarism, and Nonprofit Organizations.* Baltimore, Md.: Johns Hopkins University Press, 1992.

Loessin, B. A., Duronio, M. A., and Borton, G. L. "Understanding Fund-Raising Effectiveness in Higher Education: Laying a Foundation." Final report prepared for the Exxon Education Foundation, 1988.

Rooney, P. M. "A Better Method for Analyzing the Costs and Benefits of Fundraising at Universities." *Nonprofit Management and Leadership*, 1999, *10*(1), 39–56.

Schaeffer, E. "Getting the Most Out of Student Callers." *Fund Raising Management*, 1990, *21*(4), 46-49.

Tanner, N. N., and Ramsey, P. "Raising Money for Women from Women: The Story of a Successful Campaign." New Directions for Philanthropic Fundraising, no. 2. San Francisco: Jossey-Bass, 1993.

JODY ABZUG *is director of the Campaign for Neighborhood Music School in New Haven. She has been in the development field since 1993 and has worked for Columbia University School of Law, Wesleyan University, Hamden Hall Country Day School, Hadassah, and the Women's Zionist Organization of America; as a consultant for Nonprofit Strategies Group; and as an independent consultant. A 1988 graduate of Williams College, she lives on the Choate campus with husband Jim, a school administrator, and their four-year-old twins.*

RIKKI ABZUG, *who has a doctorate in organizational sociology from Yale University, is assistant professor of nonprofit management at the Milano Graduate School of Management and Urban Policy, New School University. Abzug, a former associate director of Yale University's Program on Nonprofit Organizations, is a 1986 graduate of Swarthmore College. She lives in New Jersey with her husband, Patrick Brady, a surrealist painter, and their two beautiful daughters.*

The Everybody Wins! Foundation (EW!) was at a crossroads in 2000. Through a million-dollar grant, the U.S. Department of Education was funding a nationwide replication of EW!'s successful literacy and mentoring program. As a result, EW!'s founder separated from the original operation to lead the nationwide expansion of Everybody Wins! USA, and an executive director was hired to spearhead the prototype program, now called Everybody Wins! Metro New York.

7

Orchestrating change by empowering volunteer fundraisers: A case study

Alan Jones, Angela Loguercio, Arthur Makar

A CHALLENGE FACING EVERY new nonprofit executive director is how best to make use of his or her talents and expertise to put a personal imprimatur on the new organization while respecting and building upon the predecessors' foundations. This can be an even greater challenge when the executive director replaces an organization's founder.

Up to the point where the first paid leader is hired, an organization, its programs, and its people have been led by a single vision. Founder's Syndrome is a resulting complication faced by an incoming executive director.

NEW DIRECTIONS FOR PHILANTHROPIC FUNDRAISING, NO. 39, SPRING 2003 © WILEY PERIODICALS, INC.

Founder's Syndrome "occurs when, rather than working toward its overall mission, the organization operates primarily according to the personality of a prominent person in the organization." [It is considered to be] "primarily an organizational problem—not . . . of the person in the prominent position" (McNamara, 2001). The question that this raises, however, is: How does an organization, especially one with symptoms of Founder's Syndrome, successfully transition leadership from founder to successor?

Our case study explores this question, using fundraising as a frame of reference while looking at the complementary roles played by the chief volunteer fundraiser (CVF), executive director (ED) and development director (DD) in creating a new, signature special event.

Further questions, not addressed in this case study, are: Why does EW! still need volunteers involved in fundraising? How did their roles evolve in the transition period from founder to ED?

Background information and the impetus for change

Organizational change, whether in the for-profit or nonprofit sector, does not occur in a vacuum. When orchestrating change, one has to maneuver through the organization's institutional history and its people, carefully avoiding bear traps along the way.

In EW!'s case, the founder had committed to working with another nonprofit on a collaborative fundraising event. Historically, this event provided EW! with modest income, but without the risk of assuming substantial pre-event expenditures. However, this "affordable" event came with a cost. While the majority of the expenses were incurred by the facilitating group and shared among the participating nonprofit organizations, so were the publicity and spotlight. Because of its lack of exposure in the New York City philanthropic community, this collaborative event did little to raise funding or awareness regarding EW!'s programs.

The new executive director wanted to create a stand-alone fundraising event that would do what all good events should do:

- Raise significant dollars.
- Make the best use of volunteers and their talents.
- Serve as a means to introduce new prospective donors to the organization.

Empowering the key players

The ED's allies in this endeavor were the chief volunteer fundraiser, who was of like mind, and the development director, who would assume the day-to-day implementation of this proposed event.

In his seminal book, *Designs for Fund-Raising*, Harold J. Seymour (1988) states, "Just as any good pair of scissors needs two blades, with each blade helping to keep the other sharp, so it is that any good fund-raising operation needs both kinds of leadership—the layman who leads and the staff man who manages and serves."

While the gender language is outdated, the concept is not. Successful fundraising shops have two interrelated sets of players: volunteers who govern and lead, and staff who drive the organization on a day-to-day basis. For a change in culture to occur, volunteers and staff must be synchronized. In a perfect world, volunteer leadership cultivates its peers to foster a desired result. The staff leader is significant, but change is accomplished by the governing body.

Think of a theatrical staging. You need a script, a producer, a stage manager, actors, a director, and so on. There is "front of house" and "back of house" activity. For a literacy organization, this was truly "Readers' Theatre"!

The role of staff leadership in orchestrating change is often backstage: drafting the script and providing it to volunteers, in essence setting the stage for organizational change.

To produce the new stand-alone fundraising event, the ED needed first to empower the key players in their roles: the CVF (lead actor) and the DD (stage manager). Both individuals had "performed" under the direction of the founder. The new ED had a new style and vision, yet was able to empower these players by clarifying all three roles and responsibilities within the organization.

The criteria that follow are by no means comprehensive; rather, the responsibilities presented here were critically needed to orchestrate the new event.

Roles and responsibilities of effective EDs, CVFs, and DDs

An effective executive director, in addition to leading the day-to-day operations of the organization:

- *Develops an annual fundraising plan with the CVF and DD.* The key words in this phrase are "develops" and "with." In his article entitled "The Residue of Leadership: Why Ambition Matters," James Champy (2002, p. 117) attests, "It's not easy to give up control of one's life's work. But the best way to keep control is to share it. Passion and commitment are cemented when decision-making authority and personal rewards are widely distributed."
- *Collaborates with the CVF and DD on specific fundraising activities delineated in the above plan.*
- *Facilitates board members' activities during and between meetings by providing staff leadership and sharing concise information.* Again, the prepositions in this phrase—*during, between*—provide insight into the nature of the ED's job. Much of the ED's work takes place between meetings, that is, outside of the public venue and as alluded to before, "backstage."
- *Informs the board about the work of similar organizations as well as trends and issues that may impact the organization and its services.* With his thirty years of experience in the nonprofit sector, and as a volunteer leader of the AFP Foundation Board, the new ED was credible to volunteers and well-poised to perform this task. His perspective was invaluable to a board that was well-versed in the financial and corporate sector and appreciated his own volunteer viewpoint.

- *Provides staffing for board committees and coordinates committees' activities.* These tasks, though mundane, enable board members to more easily contribute their time and expertise to the nonprofit they are serving.

The five criteria just listed serve to empower the individuals within an organization. By shifting the weight of responsibilities to others, "high achievers find ways to attain their dreams, exercise their potential, and exceed previous limitations. Enlightened leaders also give colleagues the information, authority, and resources to make their own decisions" (Champy, 2002).

With authority and support from the ED, the CVP can more effectively lead an organization's fundraising objectives when he or she:

- *Presents an annual fundraising plan to the board of directors for approval.* It is crucial that the CVF present the plan to the board. Board members are more likely to buy into and contribute to a plan that is devised and implemented by a peer member who has similar time constraints and is a volunteer.
- *Implements this fundraising plan by delegating fundraising responsibilities among key staff, the development committee, and appropriate board members.* Because this CVF had an accurate assessment of most of the board members' contacts and areas of expertise, he was able to assign particular tasks to the most appropriate members.
- *Facilitates communication among the board, ED, and DD.* Much of this communication took place "offstage," outside board meetings. The CVF often fielded questions and concerns from the board and relayed those questions to the ED.
- *Respects and encourages other board members by making efficient use of their volunteer time.* The CVF conducted development committee meetings that were focused and concise. Because the CVF kept board members abreast of new developments between meetings, no time was wasted in bringing members up to speed.

Because the CVF skillfully anticipated possible resistance from and anxieties of the board members, he was equipped to address concerns that might arise during the meetings.

Through the support of and collaboration with the ED and CVF, the DD can successfully implement and supervise the elements of a comprehensive fundraising program when he or she:

- *Supports the ED and CVF by preparing materials and providing them to board members.* The materials provided included statistics on EW!'s fundraising history, standards of measurement for special events, and realistic projections for EW!'s future funding.
- *Develops and maintains communication vehicles to enhance fundraising efforts.*
- *Maintains appropriate relationships with internal colleagues and the board so as to be well informed of both programmatic needs and funding possibilities.* Because the DD had previously worked as an EW! program staff member, she was already aware of the organization's project-funding needs and the constraints placed on the program staff, making her a knowledgeable and credible liaison between both groups.

Table 7.1 displays the intricate steps taken by the ED, CVF, and DD to secure the board's buy-in on the new event. The shaded areas represent the activities that were conducted "backstage," between board and committee meetings.

Within each of the meetings, several board members showed the lingering effects of Founder's Syndrome. Their attitude was, if it ain't broke, don't fix it.

These members were wary of changing EW!'s special event fundraising strategy. According to McNamara (2003), such issues are common to an organization suffering from Founder's Syndrome. Individuals often "have a very difficult time letting go of the strategies that worked to quickly grow the organization, despite evidence that the organization can no longer absorb this rapid growth without major changes."

Table 7.1. Leadership triangle in action

	Board Fundraising Chair (BFC)	Chief Executive Officer (CEO)	Chief Development Officer (CDO)
Prior to Initial Meeting	• Scheduled meeting to initiate independent special event	• Collaborated with BFC to develop strategies	• Worked with CEO to gather historical budget information
First Meeting	• Chaired development meeting • Provided his and other board members' perspective on past events • Elicited board members' concerns over launching solo fundraising event	• Expressed options for event that incorporated past nonprofit experience	• Presented historical budget information to the board
Between 1st & 2nd Meetings	• Asked CEO to garner data and relevant articles to address board members' concerns	• Gathered and analyzed data and relevant articles to address board members' concerns	
Second Meeting	• Empowered CEO to speak with event planners	• Met with Susan Ulin Associates (SUA) to discuss possibility of managing EW! event	
Between 2nd & 3rd Meetings	• Received information from CEO & CDO • Discussed strategy to obtain majority vote to hold our own event	• Evaluated information from SUA and other nonprofit event income statements to make recommendation to board • Developed revenue projections based on income/expense ratio	• Distributed projections to all other board members

Table 7.1. (*continued*)

	Board Fundraising Chair (BFC)	Chief Executive Officer (CEO)	Chief Development Officer (CDO)
Third Meeting	• Convened meeting • Addressed board member's initial concerns while expressing his recommendation for EW! to host its own event		• Fielded questions from board of directors regarding the work of the development committee
	• Received unanimous vote from board of directors to host our own event		
After 3rd Meeting	• Discussed role in identification and solicitation of additional co-chair	• Lined up high-profile board member as co-chair of EW! event • With participating board member, secured major personality as honorary co-chair	• Developed Event Prospectus material for potential co-chair(s)

Table 7.2 includes actual quotes of board members expressed during board and committee meetings and recorded in the minutes. The quotes are categorized as either "reactive" or "proactive." The fourth column lists the final results of the inaugural gala.

As displayed in Table 7.1, EW!'s new signature event was, by any measure, a phenomenal success, but especially financially and programmatically. Perhaps the best anecdotal evidence of the event's success was the vocal, on-the-record support of the founder himself.

In a December 19, 2002, article featured in *The Chronicle of Philanthropy,* founder Arthur Tannenbaum expressed his "jubilation that the inaugural gala proved that the EW! Foundation now had the governance structure and skills needed to raise significant revenue for program expansion" (Welner, 2002).

Conclusion

Successful organizations, both nonprofit and for-profit, are only as good as their dual leadership sets. Leadership is a fluid concept that flows between volunteer leadership and senior management. Staff implement the directives of a governing body.

When power is in transition, particularly from the founder to a new chief executive, it is critical that every leadership player be strong, focused, and well-defined so that all members recognize their individual expected outcomes, plus how their work together and separately must mesh to create a cohesive whole.

References

Champy, J. "The Residue of Leadership: Why Ambition Matters." In F. Hesselbein and R. Johnston (eds.), *On Creativity, Innovation, and Renewal.* San Francisco: Jossey-Bass, 2002.

McNamara, C. "Founders' Syndrome: How Corporations Suffer—and Can Recover (for Nonprofit and For-Profit Organizations)." *The Difference: DRG Quarterly Webzine, 1*(2), 2001. Retrieved February 5, 2003, from [http://www.e-thedifference.com/Issue_2/founders_syndrome.html]

Seymour, H. J. *Designs for Fund-Raising.* (2nd ed.) Ambler, Pa.: Balthauser North American, 1988.

Table 7.2. Highlights from board and committee meetings

	Reactive	Proactive	Results
Financial Concerns	"What additional revenue would result from this new event as compared to prior Youth Inc. events?"	"Let's be conservative and say none in the first year. But in future years we will raise more."	The EW! Metro NY Inaugural Gala was a financial success that raised more money that we had with Youth Inc. in years past."
	"Can we afford to take a risk of a 'wash' this year?"	"We must be willing to accept the risk."	Our event attracted many new donors who have been added to our database.
		"The event will empower us in the long term to raise more money."	The event was not only a financial success but also a qualitative one. Four high-profile celebrities read literary excerpts to a captive audience of over 300 attendees at the Waldorf-Astoria. The founder and his wife were honored with a National Points of Light award. The evening allowed EW! Metro NY the time and space to deliver its own message.
	"We will not raise enough money to justify our costs."	"This will be a quality event. The difference in doing the event may not be quantitative this year, but there will be a great qualitative difference."	
Fear of Change	"We don't know how to put together an event like this."	"We will learn from mistakes this year. We may be worse off the first year, but in years hence we will reap the benefits of a successful fundraiser that truly reflects the spirit and caliber of the organization."	

"Youth Inc. has been very helpful to us. We should be loyal to them."

"Board members and high-end donors don't come to these events anyway. Why should we spend 35 percent of gross revenue on a upscale event?"

"We must separate if we want to build our own brand loyalty and constituency."

"We need an upscale event to attract upscale donors and board members."
"A high-end event establishes us out of the block. Holding a low-end event runs the risk of losing supporters."
"This event will allow board members an avenue to showcase our program as well as give and solicit donations."

In addition to attracting new donors, EW! received positive press in several publications, including the *NY Times* and *The Chronicle of Philanthropy*.

Our inaugural gala increased the participation of and renewed a sense of pride among our board members. The majority of our board and many of the targeted upscale donors attended the event. Several of the new donors have told us they are looking forward to our event next year.

Welner, A.S. "A Nonprofit Group Helps Tiny New York Charities Drum Up Big Fund-Raising Galas" *The Chronicle of Philanthropy*, Dec. 19, 2002.

ALAN JONES *is board member and chair of development at Everybody Wins! He is also managing director and co-head of the Financial Sponsors Group at Morgan Stanley in New York City, director of Physicians for Human Rights, chief fund agent for the Harvard Business School Class of 1987, a fundraiser for the Brearly School, a member of the Investment Committee of the Unitarian Church of All Souls in New York, and chairman of the All Souls Emergency Relief Fund.*

ANGELA LOGUERCIO *is development associate for Everybody Wins! She researches potential sources of funding, writes grant proposals to corporate and private foundations, and edits the organization's newsletter. She was previously the program coordinator for Everybody Wins! where she coordinated literacy and mentoring programs at six New York City Elementary schools for over 500 students and volunteers from various organizations, including Goldman, Sachs & Co. and The New York Mets.*

ARTHUR MAKAR *is executive director of Everybody Wins! He has spent thirty years in the nonprofit sector. Prior to assuming his position with Everybody Wins!, he spent six years with the American Lung Association (ALA) as senior director of Major & Planned Gifts for the national organization and as CEO of the ALA of Queens. He holds a Baccalaureate degree from Boston College, a Masters of Science in Education from Suffolk University and is a Certified Fund Raising Executive (CFRE). He also serves on the Association of Fund Raising Professionals (AFP) Foundation Board of Directors and Corporate Advisory Board for the National Association of Drug Abuse Programs (NADAP).*

Index

Back Issue/Subscription Order Form

Copy or detach and send to:
Jossey-Bass, 989 Market Street, San Francisco, CA 94103-1741

Call or fax toll free!
Phone 888-378-2537 6AM-5PM PST; Fax 888-481-2665

Back issues: Please send me the following issues at $28 each
(Important: please include series initials and issue number, such as PF10)

1. PF _____

_____

_____

$ _____ Total for single issues

$ _____ SHIPPING CHARGES: SURFACE   Domestic   Canadian

		SURFACE	Domestic	Canadian
	First Item		$5.00	$6.00
	Each Add'l Item		$3.00	$1.50

For next-day and second-day delivery rates, call the number listed above.

Subscriptions   Please ❑ start ❑ renew my subscription to *New Directions for Philanthropic Fundraising* at the following rate:

US: ❑ Individual $99   ❑ Institutional $199
Canada: ❑ Individual $99   ❑ Institutional $239
All others: ❑ Individual $123   ❑ Institutional $273

NOTE: Issues are published quarterly. Subscriptions are for the calendar year only. Subscriptions begin with the Spring issue. Add appropriate sales tax for your state for single issue orders. No sales tax for U.S. subscriptions.

$ _____ Total single issues and subscriptions (Canadian residents, add GST for subscriptions and single issues)

❑ Payment enclosed (U.S. check or money order only)

❑ VISA, MC, AmEx # _____ Exp. date _____

Signature _____ Day phone _____

❑ Bill me (U.S. institutional orders only. Purchase order required)

Purchase order # _____

Federal Tax ID 135593032   GST 89102-8052

Name _____

Address _____

_____

Phone _____ E-mail _____

For more information about Jossey-Bass, visit our Web site at:
www.josseybass.com   **PRIORITY CODE = ND1**

Previous Issues Available